"John Delaney has assembled 20 engaging, engrossing by prominent men and women who write intimately o saint who affects their lives. . . . The book is eminently valuable. . . . A rewarding treasury of spiritual reading for any season."     —*The Critic*

"There are some very practical insights and some interesting personal stories here—and some surprises, more than enough to have justified this effort to make the saints come alive again for our day."     —*Spiritual Book News*

"Because of the quality writing—much of it personal, all of it graceful—the feeling is conveyed that perhaps devotion to the saints might not be something to hide after all. If a gathering of intellectuals can dare come out of the closet and tell us they take the saints seriously, then perh— the rest of us can begin to stir also. . . . [a] sple—

                                                                    *olic Reporter*

". . . coul                                                         terpart to the
venerable,                                                          'Lives of the
Saints.'"

"The sketche                                      however mystical the
subjects; many                          e recent past both enliven and
relax the accou        n form as well as in expressed intention, the collection allows a nice interplay between past and present and between piety and critical consciousness. . . . An image slowly forms itself in the book, of a communio sanctorum here on earth . . . ever old and ever new. *Saints for All Seasons* celebrates this community as it celebrates those who have gone on ahead. It is nice to see such piety back in print."     —*America*

". . . makes worthwhile reading for all, non-believers included."     —*Publishers Weekly*

"Seldom have I read an anthology of such even excellence."     —*The Cord*

# Saints for All Seasons

# SAINTS
# FOR ALL
# SEASONS

John J. Delaney, editor

COMPLETE AND UNABRIDGED

Image Books
A Division of Doubleday & Company, Inc.
Garden City, New York

Image Book edition published March, 1979
by special arrangement with
Doubleday & Company, Inc.

Grateful acknowledgment is made for permission to include excerpts
from the following copyrighted publications:

Excerpt from *St. John of the Cross: His Life and Poetry* by Gerald
Brenan. Reprinted by permission of Cambridge University Press.

"Crucifixion" from *Spirit Magazine*. Reprinted by permission of the
publisher.

ISBN: 0-385-12909-2

*To*
*my one love—Ann*
*who never believed the saints could ever be irrelevant*

# Contents

Introduction
13

MARY
Mary Carson
19

JUDE
Donald J. Thorman
29

PETER
Barrett McGurn
39

PAUL
E. E. Y. Hales
47

AUGUSTINE
Anne Fremantle
57

PATRICK
Gary MacEoin
67

THOMAS BECKET
Joel Wells
79

DOMINIC
Tere Rios Versace
89

FRANCIS OF ASSISI
John S. Kennedy
99

JOAN OF ARC
Candida Lund
109

THOMAS MORE
Dan Herr
119

IGNATIUS LOYOLA
John B. Breslin, S.J.
129

TERESA OF ÁVILA
Mary Purcell
141

JOHN OF THE CROSS
Thomas P. McDonnell
153

FRANCIS DE SALES
John Deedy
165

VINCENT DE PAUL
Julie Kernan
175

ANNE-MARIE JAVOUHEY
Glenn Kittler
185

ANTHONY CLARET
Robert E. Burns
193

THÉRÈSE OF LISIEUX
Naomi Burton Stone
203

THE UNKNOWN SAINT
Fulton Oursler, Jr.
213

Biographies of the Contributors
221

# Introduction

Through the centuries, veneration of the saints has been a prominent feature of life in the Church. From the earliest days of Christianity men and women of great holiness have been honored by their fellow Christians for the lives they have lived and the example they have set in their quest for a spirituality that would bring them close to God in this life. These holy Christians have come from all walks of life, from lowliest beggar to all-powerful emperor, king, or queen. For just as Christ preached the good news of salvation to all, so, too, those who followed his example in their lives and have been proclaimed holy have come from all walks of life.

It is an unfortunate fact of modern life that along with other worthy practices the veneration of saints in contemporary times has fallen if not into disrepute at least into disuse. No longer do the saints have the hold and impact on us that was so prevalent as recently as a decade or so ago.

The reasons for this state of affairs are not too difficult to understand, though one does not have to agree with them. The skepticism and cynicism of the '60s have left a deep mark even on those who never assented to the philosophy of that embittered and disillusioned decade. The novel idea advanced then that the "now" was all and history had nothing to offer since all knowledge had been instantaneously acquired "now" had subconscious effects on all in view of the undeniably amazing accumulation of information in the twentieth century (the accumulation of wisdom is something else again). The study of history and philosophy declined, as subjects that had nothing to offer to today's students. With this trend went an increasing lack of interest in historical figures and what they had to offer. The saints were only one of a group affected by this attitude.

Also, it is true that there are many saints whose activities are simply unbelievable to one living in the twentieth century. They are products of their times, incomprehensible without an intimate knowledge of the customs, practices, and culture of the times in which they lived. Even with such information, we often find it difficult to understand what they did. And let's face it, some of the actions and some of the "miracles" attributed to some of the saints are simply ludicrous, a concoction of myth and the vivid imagination of fevered followers. Few people fully realize that the painstaking process and scrupulous, scientific investigation required for a modern canonization is of comparatively recent origin; many saints of early times were so proclaimed by small local cults with no attempt at all at impartial study of the claims advanced. Small wonder that so many, particularly younger people, dismissed the whole lot as not worthy of any attention at all, much less of respect, emulation, and even veneration.

This loss of respect for the saints is a great pity, for there are saints whose lives and activities can be of great value to all. The attitude toward the saints today reminds me of the attitude toward spiritual reading that prevailed just a few short years ago. Fed up with so much of the pious pap that passed for spiritual writing in the '30s, '40s and '50s, people just stopped reading all spiritual works, including the great Christian classics. As time went on, people realized that they had thrown out the baby with the bath water. Today, truly authentic spiritual writing, including or, better said, led by the great Christian spiritual classics, is more popular today than at any other time in this century, as people have again discovered the timeless treasures of Augustine, Teresa of Ávila, John of the Cross, Thomas à Kempis, and the other giants of Christian spirituality. For truly great spirituality transcends time and geography, was valid in past centuries, is valid now, and will be in centuries ahead.

And so it is and will be with the saints. Some saints are just not appropriate for today. Some are merely local cult figures who have never been subjected to the rigorous scrutiny that the Church today requires for canonization. Some were built up by unscrupulous promoters. Some are products of a culture foreign to our own. But remember, no one is obliged to venerate any saint he or she does not wish to. The Church has never declared the veneration of any saint a matter of faith, necessary for salvation. What she does say in canonizing a saint is that the person declared to be a saint is worthy of veneration. Indeed objections to the saints included in the calendar of the saints are minuscule compared to the uproar caused when Church authorities attempt to remove saints from the official calendar, as witness the resentment expressed a few years ago when certain saints were removed because information about them was too scanty or was unauthenticated!

But if there are saints not appropriate for today's believers, there are many whose example and lives are still most appropriate for the chaotic and disturbing age in which we live. Just as in the literature of spirituality there are works whose intrinsic merits are such as to have universal and timeless appeal, so there are saintly individuals who offer inspiration and whose lives can serve as examples for us today just as they did in their own times. We are so wrapped up in the complex problems of today's world that we have a tendency to overlook the fact that men and women have faced many of those same problems, though in different settings, in other times. The wisdom and insights they applied to face those challenges are still fresh and relevant today. Knowledge changes as we expand our horizons, but true wisdom is timeless and universal.

Ah, yes, there are things we can learn from the past, and who can better be of assistance to us in facing the spiritual and even material dilemmas that constantly confront mankind than those saints whose complete trust in God has al-

ways provided guidance and inspiration? Saints for all seasons? Of course there are.

The purpose of this book, then, is to call to your attention
twenty men and women whose lives can provide inspiration
and example for those trying to follow Christ today as best
they can. They are real, flesh-and-blood people, human beings
with the same weaknesses we all possess as human beings but
with an inner strength and purposefulness that can serve as
examples to us today in the daily struggle that is life.

For this purpose, I approached twenty distinguished authors and journalists and asked each of them to select the
saint who had most affected his or her life and write of that
saint in terms of that saint's appeal today. They here offer a
varied assortment of men and women ranging from apostolic
times to the present, some famous, some quite obscure; there
is even one about the Unknown Saint. I think you will find
all of them interesting, and in some cases they will give you
entirely new insights into well-known figures. In any event I
trust you will agree, after reading about them, that these
saints are not museum pieces from history but men and
women you will enjoy knowing today—saints for all seasons.

JOHN J. DELANEY

*Editor's note:* For the reader's benefit I have provided a short
factual biography of each saint at the beginning of each article; also,
at the end of the book, I have provided short biographical sketches
of each of the contributors. These biographies, both of saints and of
contributors, are solely my responsibility. The feast day of each saint
is the date of his or her death unless otherwise indicated at the end
of his or her biography.

J.J.D.

# Saints for All Seasons

# Mary—Mother and Friend

## (FIRST CENTURY)

## MARY CARSON

*There is little genuine information about the life and person of Mary. What we know of her is to be found in the New Testament, and it is from the biblical data that the role of Mary in the Church has been developed. Although of course she plays a prominent role in the infancy narratives (Matthew 1:18–2:23 and Luke 1:5–2:52), there are only scattered references to her elsewhere in the New Testament. How authentic this information is has been the subject of prolonged study by biblical scholars. But the infancy narratives clearly and unequivocally declare her divine maternity, Jesus' messianic character, and Mary's virginity. Nothing is known of her childhood, though tradition has it that she was the daughter of Joachim and Anne, was born in Jerusalem, as a child was presented in the Temple by her parents, and took a vow of perpetual virginity. According to the evangelists, she was betrothed to Joseph and was visited by the angel Gabriel, who announced to her that she was to be the mother of Jesus. She became pregnant of the Holy Spirit and then married Joseph after he was assured by an angel that "she has conceived what is in her by the Holy Spirit" (Matthew 1:20).*

*Soon after, she visited her cousin Elizabeth, who was bearing
John. Shortly after Jesus' birth, in Bethlehem, she and Joseph
were forced to flee with Jesus to Egypt to escape the wrath of
Herod, who feared the child as a rival for his throne. On
Herod's death they returned and settled at Nazareth. Nothing is known of her life there except Jesus' presentation in
the Temple (Luke 2:22) and an incident recounted in Luke
2:41–50 in which Mary and Joseph lost Jesus on the
way home and found him discoursing learnedly with the doctors in the Temple. Mary was instrumental in getting Jesus to
perform his first miracle, changing water into wine at Cana
(John 2:1–5), and then returned to Capernaum with him
(John 2:12), which may mean she no longer lived in Nazareth. There are references to her as the mother of Jesus in
Matthew 13:55 and Mark 6:3, and she is again mentioned in
Matthew 12:46–50, Mark 3:31–35, and Luke 8:19–21, when
Christ describes his "mother and brothers" as "anyone who
does the will of God." She is described as being at the
Crucifixion (but only in John 19:25–27), when she was given
into John's care, which would seem to indicate she had no
relatives to take care of her. She was with the disciples in
Jerusalem in the days before Pentecost (Acts 1:14), but there
is no further mention of her in the New Testament. According to tradition, she went to live in Ephesus with John,
where she died, but another tradition has her living in Jerusalem until her death.*

My relationship with the Blessed Mother has changed over
the years. As a first grader in Catholic elementary school, during the early 1940s, that relationship was distant—a small
child hero-worshiping an idol. To me, Mary was an ethereal
goddess on a pedestal.

Now, in the late 1970s, the mother of eight children, I
regard the mother of Jesus as my good friend. She is as close
to me as my favorite neighbor.

My earliest memories of Mary consist of collecting holy

cards and trying to imitate her by saying pious rosaries and planning to be a nun. Later, when I was about eight, I read *Lovely Lady Dressed in Blue* and became impressed with Mary's motherhood.

I decided it would be nice if I had a child . . . just as Mary did. I understood that God usually sent babies to homes with a mother and father. But since He sent Jesus to Mary the way He did, I thought if I prayed hard enough He'd send me a little boy. God didn't answer my prayer. I was disappointed. It was some time before I understood that prayer alone cannot accomplish some things.

My knowledge of the Blessed Mother grew slowly as I was encouraged in devotion to my "name saint," made the mandatory novenas, and wore a miraculous medal. I coasted into my teens, deeply committed to the Blessed Mother—committed to a plaster image that had a direct line to God's ear.

After high school, I asked her daily to take care of my fiancé, to bring him back safely from the war in Korea. She did. When he returned, we were married and God began answering that earlier prayer. He sent a little boy . . . and another . . . and another . . . and five sisters for them.

During those years, I found my devotion to Mary changing. I thought I was losing it. I no longer had that all-trusting "rabbit's foot" belief in her. I still prayed, but not as frequently and more from habit than devotion. I seemed unable to "imitate" her. I still had that picture of her as a spirit—above and apart from everyday cares. And with a house full of small children I had a great many daily cares.

I made a weekend retreat. The retreat master devoted one of his lectures to the Blessed Mother and what little we actually know of her from the Gospels. He touched, a bit, on her humanity. It started me thinking. I began to understand what was said in those Gospels, to consider what Mary's life must really have been. I read Henri Daniel-Rops' book *Daily Life in the Time of Jesus* for background.

Her home probably was a one-room structure divided by a half wall. The animals lived on one side of the wall, the people on the other. The warmth from the animals helped heat the home. Comparing her home with mine, I realized Mary must have been a pretty rugged, resilient, resourceful woman —just to make a go of things in those conditions.

I continued to develop an image of her, something I could relate to. The first mention of Mary in the Gospels is at the Annunciation. She was afraid. "Afraid" must have been an understatement. If someone in a white robe appeared in my room and told me I was pregnant—but don't worry about it— I'd be terrified.

Then Mary did something women so often do. There was no sense to what the angel was telling her, yet she made a wholehearted commitment to her Beloved. How often women go ahead with full confidence just because they love someone!

I remember the first time I did it. My husband-to-be was in Korea when the war ended. Instead of waiting to get married till the tour of duty in Korea was over, he had an idea. He would re-enlist so he could transfer to Japan, fly home, marry me, and we'd fly back to live in Japan. He telephoned me from Japan, where he was on leave, and suggested the plan to me.

Thinking back now, it was absurd. We hadn't seen each other in over a year. I was only nineteen, knew nothing about living in a foreign country, and was extremely close to my family. But did I hesitate? No. I agreed immediately to go with him. It made no sense, yet I had so much love for him that, somehow, it would be okay. As it turned out, he couldn't get the transfer, so we got married when he returned to the United States.

Every time women give themselves wholeheartedly to their beloved, they are imitating Mary's example at the Annunciation.

Then what did Mary do? When she found out she was pregnant, she ran to tell her cousin. And in telling Elizabeth, she again did something so typical of women. She gave God the credit for her joy. Women tend to find their joy vi-

cariously. I am happy because I have a marvelous husband, a
beautiful family. Mary was happy because God had blessed
her.

Women also can lose track of time. I run over to visit a
friend for a minute and stay an hour. I'm ready to leave, and
there are half a dozen more things I must share with my
friend. Mary went to tell Elizabeth she was pregnant—and
stayed for three months.

Something else about Mary's pregnancy fascinates me.
What was her parents' reaction? Anne and Joachim are the
names tradition assigns them. When Mary explained to them
that she was pregnant and going off on a ninety-mile trip
with Joseph—who wasn't her husband or the father of the
Child—how did they take it?

How would *you* if it were *your* daughter?

Yet, somehow, they let her go. Is there a lesson in this for
those of us who, as parents, must accept things from our children that make no sense? Mary was only a young girl—a teen-
ager. . . . What confidence Joachim and Anne must have
had in her!

Mary's trip to Bethlehem must have been an ordeal.
Christmas cards always show her in spotless blue robes, riding
serenely on a donkey. What was it really like for her? The
distance was about the same as it is from New York to Phila-
delphia. By donkey, it would have to have taken them at
least a week. A week . . . in the later months of pregnancy
. . . on a donkey . . . with no McDonald's or hot showers
along the way. . . .

I made a trip once in late pregnancy and was absolutely
miserable. My baby-to-be spent the entire trip doing calisthen-
ics—isometrics against my ribs and bladder. I was riding in
a car. . . .

And when Mary and Joseph got to Bethlehem, what was
she thinking as they went from inn to inn—and couldn't find a
place to stay? How often we're caught in a situation that
seems desperate—no possible solution—and each time we try,
we are rebuffed again. . . .

Paintings of the Nativity show Mary kneeling piously by the manger, created, I am sure, by artists who didn't have the faintest idea how a woman feels immediately after childbirth. After the ninety-mile trip by donkey and having given birth unattended, in a stable, she must have been exhausted. More likely she curled up in Joseph's cloak, her Baby wrapped against her to keep Him warm . . . and slept.

But how much rest did she get? No sooner had she given birth than company started coming. Those shepherds . . . and those angels singing all night. . . . Did she wish things would just quiet down a bit, so she could get some sleep? I can remember times after I came home from the hospital with a new baby when I wanted to rest but company stopped in. At least they didn't stay all night. I know how Mary must have felt.

She had no disposable diapers, either. Remember the swaddling clothes? I always thought that just meant nice, warm baby clothes. I found out that swaddling clothes were long strips of fabric in which the baby was wound, something like a mummy. It was done so the baby's legs would grow straight. But can you imagine having to unwind a baby every time a change was necessary?

Then Mary took Him out to show Him off: the Presentation. Don't all mothers do the same? And Mary believed the things said concerning Him. . . . We dress our babies in their finest, show them off . . . and believe all the marvelous things predicted for them. Because that's how mothers are.

Few mothers experience a direct threat to their children's lives, but there are other threats—drugs, alcohol, bad company—that can "kill" our children. In these fears we can gain some understanding of Mary's feelings when she took Jesus and fled to Egypt—fled for His life.

And what were her feelings when she discovered He was missing from the caravan returning from Jerusalem? She knew the road could be dangerous. Both thieves and wild animals could be encountered.

I've been through a similar experience. I know the icy fear

that can grip a mother's heart. One evening, I called the children in—and one little daughter was missing. It was growing dark. The whole neighborhood joined in the search—through the house, through every other yard, through nearby vacant lots. A neighbor's boy came to me: "I just checked the canal. I didn't see her floatin', so I guess she didn't drown."

We called the police. They sent a car to help. One more search of the house, and we found her: fast asleep on her bed, rolled in a quilt.

When I lost that child, the moment I got her back was awful. I was so thrilled to have her safe I wanted to scoop her into my arms and love her to death. But I had been so upset that I was ready to murder her for the worry I'd been through.

I didn't know whether to kiss her or kill her . . . or both.

Mary's conversation with Jesus when she found Him in the Temple, as reported in the Gospels, seems unreal. I could believe it more readily if she took Jesus by the scruff of the neck and marched Him back home.

And what was Jesus' reaction? "Why were you worrying?" How often our children have no grasp at all of the worry they cause us, and give us a quick answer that hurts worse than the worry!

Where did the Gospel stories about Jesus' birth and early years come from? The Evangelists were not present to record the events personally. I feel these stories must have been told originally by Mary herself.

Isn't it interesting that, from the time He was twelve, when she found Him in the Temple, until He was an adult, the Gospels say nothing of Jesus? What about His teen years? It's almost as though Mary didn't want to talk about Jesus as a teen-ager.

Raising teen-agers can be a difficult job. How impossible for us to convince them that we know what's best! Was it any different with Jesus? Teens are usually convinced they know everything. What was it like trying to raise one who really did?

Or did He?

Were they fully conscious all the time that He was God? I doubt it. I think that much of that time their lives were quite ordinary.

Two of my eight children are "special." One is brain-injured, the other mentally retarded. There are many times I am conscious of their lives' being extraordinary. The fact that the brain-injured child is alive is a miracle. She was so severely injured in an accident that she should have died. And the wonder of that can be awe-inspiring at times.

But, most of the time, these children just fall into the regular routine of family living. I believe that it was so with Mary and Jesus, too.

The wedding at Cana is the next time the Gospel mentions Mary. Why did she notice they had run out of wine? Because women tend to observe little things? And try to prevent others' embarrassment?

Years earlier, in the Temple, Jesus had wanted to get into His Father's business and Mary had said He wasn't ready. Now, at Cana, by asking Him for a miracle, she acknowledged it was time.

That break—her Child grown and on His own. . . . What of her? She must have had the same thoughts all mothers have, the bittersweet aloneness.

Oftentimes our children say things that hurt deeply. Usually what they say is not what they mean, but the words sting anyway. There is a story in the Gospel about Jesus preaching and someone mentioning to Him that His Mother was looking for Him. He said, "Who is My Mother?" We are told it was His way of showing that He was brother to all of us. But I'll bet those words cut deeply when she heard them.

The Gospel doesn't mention Mary that first Palm Sunday. Did she thrill to the praise He was receiving? Mothers are proud of their children's accomplishments. She must have been.

And what of the Passion: the Agony, the trial? Mary isn't mentioned in the Gospel accounts until the Crucifixion.

My own belief is that Mary must not have known of Jesus' arrest. From what we know of her, she was a strong, deeply loving mother. I cannot picture her standing docilely by, allowing the abuse of her Son, without protest. If she had known, she would have been there. The Gospels would have mentioned it, because she would have tried to protect Him as a mother tiger would protect her cub.

As she stood beneath the cross, what was she thinking? At that moment, could she have believed He was God? Could she have been sure? Her Son—convicted as a criminal—dead on a cross. His dreams, His goals, His ideals, all apparently futile.

Can we ever have a problem that she can't understand?

When they took Him down from the cross and she held Him for the last time, what were her thoughts? I once held the almost-lifeless body of my daughter after her accident. . . . It was the ultimate emptiness for a mother. But my daughter recovered.

What of Mary? He was dead. She had given Him life. He was flesh of her flesh. He was to have been the Messiah, the Son of God. . . . The executed criminal. . . .

She must have cried the parched sobs of total loss of all she had lived for. On Good Friday she didn't know there would be an Easter Sunday.

How could she continue to believe? Certainly not by any logical sense. But she did—when others turned away. A woman's indomitable faith. . . .

I find whatever problems I face with my children . . . whatever joys . . . I can talk to Mary about them. She's been there. She understands. She consoles during the heartaches, delights in the accomplishments—and laughs at the antics.

She's my close friend. We can all regard her that way.

It's easy to go to her with problems. Whatever difficulties we face, no matter how desperate, we can talk to her about them. She knows. She understands. She'll help.

# Jude

## (FIRST CENTURY)

## DONALD J. THORMAN

*Little is known about Jude. Listed in Luke as one of the Twelve, he is not so listed in Matthew and Mark, though a Thaddeus is. Most Biblicists agree that Jude and Thaddeus are the same. In the canonical Gospel of Jude, he identifies himself as Jude the brother of James (probably the Less). Whether the Jude of Luke is the same as the author of the epistle of Jude is disputed by biblical scholars. Tradition has it that he preached in Mesopotamia and then joined Simon in Persia, where he was martyred. Despite the paucity of information about him, he has been widely venerated for centuries as the patron saint of desperate situations and hopeless causes. His feast day is celebrated October 28.*

"Why," a friend asked, "would you choose to write about Jude, probably the least known of the saints and apostles and about whom there is so little information?"

Thereby, as they say, hangs a tale.

Before 1951, I had no substantial recollection of Jude. But, that year, I was away in graduate school at Fordham Univer-

sity when serious illness in the family made it seem impera-
tive for me to return home to the Midwest. It was a scary
thought for me, I must confess. I was so close to completing
my doctoral work, but duty seemed to demand a return. Yet,
I had no job and no special prospects.

Then, providentially, during my return home at Christmas,
1951, a friend told me the *Voice of St. Jude* magazine (now
*U. S. Catholic*) was looking for an editor. Having done some
reporting and writing for the previous four years, I asked for
an interview and was granted one by the late Claretian Father Joachim DePrada and the business manager, Robert E.
Burns. Shortly after my return to New York, they offered me
the position, to begin at the earliest date. Thanks to the
Fordham faculty I was able to take my mid-term examina-
tions early and began work as managing editor of the *Voice
of St. Jude* in January 1952, a position I held until April
1956.

It was during this period that Jude became a part of my
life. One of the features of the publication at that time was
"St. Jude's Mail," which was made up of letters from grateful
clients of the Saint of the Impossible for favors received
through his intercession. It was my task to read all the mail,
evaluate it, and condense it for publication.

I must confess I was something of a cynic about it at first,
recognizing that here and there "cures" could have been coin-
cidences or that emotional problems might be involved. Yet,
after a couple of years it became quite apparent to me that
unexplainable forces often were at work. All those people
"out there" often had nowhere else to turn, so they turned to
the Saint of Desperate Cases and, whatever the reason, they
were healed or were able to handle life and death and hard-
ship and all the exigencies of daily living with which human
beings must cope in order to survive the perils of life in a
hazardous world.

They were not "nuts" or "crazies." Some inexplicable
things did happen. And having had the opportunity to meet
face to face with some of the more difficult cases—one fine

man, for example, who had had cancer and no longer had any trace of it—I knew their devotion to Jude had put them in touch with powers higher than the human.

To Father DePrada's great credit, not one of the annual novenas began in which he did not point out the relationship between Jude the apostle and Jesus, the Master.

We honor the saints and pray to them because of their closeness to Christ, and in their own way they help give us models for imitation of how others have followed the Master. An Episcopal friend recently asked if I thought there was any need for saints today in the church—that is, Saints with a capital S. I would answer with a qualified yes.

I can well appreciate the non-Roman Catholic fear of the erratic and perhaps even idolatrous practices that were part and parcel of everyday pious Catholicism at the Reformation period. Even today some Marian devotions suffer from excesses. But none of these is my idea of a relationship to a S(s)aint.

Personally, it is little more than interesting historical information to know about Catherine of Siena's living almost solely on the Eucharist in the last days of her life or hair shirts or self-flagellation or even Barbara's double mastectomy. This is the latter half of the 1970s, and we all know of many who have all they can handle just to drag themselves from bed in the morning to catch the 7:05 to the city, fight the subway crowd, work under pressure all day, and go through the same travel routine to return home by six-thirty or seven that evening.

Today the grammar of self-discipline has changed its rules for most of us. The struggle to pay the mortgage, rear children in an alienated culture, take part in Cub or Boy Scout activities, and participate in community affairs and in a church community is about all any of us can manage. To add self-inflicted discipline to all those forces out there that are already beating on us would not only be more than heroic; it might also be more than we could cope with emotionally or physically. Or more than our spouses and families could deal with.

This is not meant to denigrate the heroism, dedication, or devotion of saints of earlier days. What it means for me is that I am seeking saints in my own times or of my own temperament to emulate. Luckily I've known a few personally, and they have provided more inspiration and spiritual strength for me than all of Butler's *Lives of the Saints*. They have been family men and women sometimes working in the professions or large corporations who have shared all the exigencies of the twentieth century that I face. I can identify with them and draw on their lives for spiritual and emotional nourishment when my needs are great.

We speak of the contemporary need of heroes, and somehow we have identified the heroic with the bigger-than-life person of national or international stature. In point of fact, my spiritual heroes today are people in circumstances generally similar to mine with whom I can share a similarity of life and life-style. The more remote they are from my way of life, the more difficult I generally find it to see them as models for me; indeed, the less possible it would be for me to imitate.

And true devotion to the saints does deal with imitation and modeling (to use the contemporary psychological terminology). Bossuet, the well-known French ecclesiastic, summed this up when he wrote that "the Christian must imitate that which he honors. Everything that is the object of our cut must be the model of our life. . . . This the constant tradition and doctrine of the Catholic Church, that the most essential part in honoring the saints is to imitate their examples."

At least for me, this helps answer the argument that devotion to the saints gets in the way of a closer relationship to Christ, the Father, and the Spirit. Or that saints are "short cuts" and substitutes for the development of a direct relationship with persons of the Trinity. Seeing how those who already have such a relationship live and reflect Christ in their lives can be a great help for me and all slow learners.

This is not a substitute for imitating Christ; instead, it is a learning aid, making it more real for us, who need all the help we can get, in relating to the Savior.

Of course, we don't *have* to pray to the saints; nor do I believe we are *required* to do so. But isn't it very human for us to want to know and become friends with those who know the Hero, especially if they have had firsthand contact with him or her? Don't we often relate to the friend of someone from whom we wish a favor or about whom we wish to know more in order to obtain that favor or that information? Don't we want to know more about how the Hero affected the lives of those about him in order to get more of a feel for what kind of person the Hero is? Of course we do this all the time, and I see no reason why we shouldn't do the same in the case of those whom we call saints because of their unique relationship to the supreme transcendental source of our faith.

It may seem contradictory or something of a paradox to some, but one of the reasons why I find Jude so appealing at this time in my life is that so little is known about him directly. He moves mysteriously in and out of the New Testament narrative, something of a shadowy figure in the background of the life of Jesus, even though he has been generally regarded as a cousin of Christ, and Bede opines that they may have grown up together. At least until recent developments in scriptural exegesis, he has also been generally accepted as one of the twelve apostles, though in my experience most persons are unaware of this.

In addition, his only contribution to the New Testament is a short epistle, of only a few hundred words. But what an interesting letter it is! He writes of "certain people" who have "infiltrated among you," and he describes those people as ones who "abuse anything they do not understand," noting that they "are a dangerous obstacle to your community meals, coming for the food and quite shamelessly only looking after themselves."

He also notes that "you, my dear friends, must use your most holy faith as your foundation and build on that, praying in the Holy Spirit; keep yourselves within the love of God. . . . When there are some who have doubts, reassure them; when there are some to be saved from the fire, pull them out. . . ."

I can think of so many applications of this to my life and the life of the institutional Church today. One of the greatest obstacles to the Catholic Christian community today, for example, is those who take and do not give in return (except perhaps for their money, the easiest of all things for most of us to give). And then there are those who "abuse anything they do not understand." Remember the (continuing) struggle to implement the reforms of Vatican Council II in an attempt to renew the Church?

Let the scripture scholars make what they will of my amateur exegesis, but my relationship of almost thirty years now with Jude has been an easy one, in which I have the freedom to visualize him as a person of my own times. He, too, lived in hard circumstances, not, by any means, the same as mine, but difficult in their own way. I know he faced stress and strain, perhaps even doubt and certainly difficulties in holding fast to the faith in a pagan age. I can see him as a firm, rocklike minister of the gospel in the runaway twentieth century.

But who really was Jude? I don't have the final historical and scriptural answers to those questions. Probably no one does. But you don't have to know all the facts about someone to know *who* he or she is.

Jude, we are able to infer, was a friend of God, a saint. He had made a commitment, a way of living, an attitude, a world view that is not much in vogue today. He was, like all other saints, someone who really believed Christ, who was a disciple. Tradition has it that on his last missionary journey a mob beat him to death with clubs. He is frequently depicted artistically with a club in memory of this form of martyrdom. Also associated with him as a symbol is an ax, because it is reputed that he was decapitated with an ax after being bludgeoned to death.

Two other traditional historical items are of interest here:

A flame—symbolic of the Holy Spirit—is often shown hovering over his head, indicating he is regarded as one of the apostles, on whom the Holy Spirit came down as tongues of flame.

And, finally, his body, along with that of Simon, has been at rest in St. Peter's at Rome for many centuries now, a tomb I visit at irregular intervals. We have a record, for example, that as far back as 1548 Pope Paul III granted a plenary indulgence to all those who visited his tomb on October 28, his feast day.

Here is a person to know. He had faith in God and the message of Calvary. So many of us today know the facts, have the information, but we lack the commitment to form our daily lives around that faith and that message. We have information but not education and wisdom. There is an essential difference, and that difference is what makes saints on the one hand and most of the rest of us on the other. We know techniques and strategy and perhaps even the subtleties of theology, but we lack the spirit and faith that breathe life into our inanimate knowledge.

Coincidentally, Easter approaches as I write this. Easter and fulfillment are perfectly legitimate and necessary in our lives. But what makes the Easter experience possible is our daily combat and victory over martyrdom. As Irenaeus has said (and as so many church banners proclaim), "The glory of God is man fully alive!" But man (or woman) fully human and alive is the person who has come to grips with reality: there are peak experiences and there is daily life.

What make for peak experiences are the valleys and the imprisonment in our mortal bodies from which the peak experiences release us momentarily to give us a taste of the transcendental, supernatural life. No psychotherapist (no matter how valuable and helpful he or she may be at times) can force on us the ultimate insight that self-realization comes only when we have met and conquered our enslavement to the other side of our humanity—our daily cross and the struggle to be free of mortal bondage.

All too often today we dream and feast on personal freedom, becoming the kind of person we were meant to be, taking charge of our own lives, getting it all put together, relating to other persons in a non-toxic fashion, becoming fully human and fully alive.

Make no mistake about my feelings. The various therapeutic modalities have much to offer, and the legitimate ones are even essential in terms of our self-esteem and self-concept, which are, after all, basic principles of the integrated, centered, fully human, and transcendental life. But these therapies won't solve our ultimate problems—they can only help us along the way.

One of the most helpful insights into our ultimate destiny I ever got was from a Jewish woman therapist, who told me that all kinds of women (and men) came to her seeking liberation. "They come to me," she said, "asking me to help them get their stuff together." My question to them, she related, is always, "OK, but, first, once you get it together, where do you want to take it?"

We are always like that too, always seeking Nirvana, looking for some kind of magic short cut or formula for happiness. But happiness, like sanctity, is not something we achieve or "get." It is the very struggle and pilgrimage itself that makes saints.

That is one of the main reasons Jude is my favorite saint. He apparently came to grips with himself and his faith, integrating the two vital forces of his personality into one centered whole. And because we know so little of the intimate details of his life, because of this very fact, I am free to build my own biography of him and to infer from the history of his era how much we share the same struggle.

In my life, Jude has been a vital force. I came to begin to know him during the most trying period of any young man's life. Near the age of thirty, just married, beginning my personal pilgrimage after World War II, facing all the tribulations young married men have always faced, I found him a refuge, a friend to whom I could turn in all the desperate and impossible situations common to my state in life. He was no substitute for Jesus, but he was (and is) like my own personal therapist, on whom I can unload in times of trial and who—dare I say it today?—has always interceded successfully for me, providing escape routes from the hazards of daily life in a technological age in which human beings with all their human problems must somehow cope.

As the cocreator of seven children, let me tell you there have been plenty of such times—financial, emotional, religious, occupational, and family-oriented—when every door seemed closed and every avenue of escape cut off. After twenty-five years of marriage and more vicissitudes of life than I care to remember, he remains one of the few friends who has not fallen by the wayside. He has not been a fair-weather friend; indeed, I have to keep making a conscious effort to relate to him in the good times that are also part of the human condition and are so very welcome as the peaks that give us momentary respite from the valleys. His reputation as the Saint of the Impossible, the Saint of Desperate Cases, all too often makes it easier to turn to him in times of quiet desperation than in those of celebration.

Jude, through my association with him and his friends, has taught me a good deal about myself and about the Christ in whom he and I and his friends believe. I have learned it is essential for each of us to take charge of our lives, both in the human and in the transcendental elements of which they are composed.

That is why I find his very mystery so compelling. Sometimes it is not well to know too much about someone; as is the case with so much of human life, a little mystery is still a good thing. Although he dates back to apostolic times, Jude still has much to tell us in the 1970s about life and Calvary and Easter. As a reflection of his Master, he also has some valuable lessons to offer us in terms of drawing closer to the Master. Jesus must have been a compelling figure to inspire those who knew him at first hand to offer their very lives and fortunes in his cause. No mere mortal could have convinced me, even to the point of martyrdom and death, to follow him. I don't think he could have convinced Jude either.

Jude lived his own life as I must live mine. Each of us has his or her own pilgrimage to make. But each of our lives still centers around a central figure to whom we owe our primary allegiance and in whom we believe. Jude faced a difficult and pagan world. So do we. He had his struggles and doubts and uncertainties in the face of adversity, even as you and I. He persevered, just as each of us today can do. It is good for us to have contemporary saints to know and look to for example and guidance. It is equally good to have a link with apostolic times and with those who knew Jesus when he dwelt with us on this very earth. Somehow it is a thread that draws together the past and the present, continuing the inexorable thrust of history from past to present.

For me, Jude is that thread, that link between the common man of apostolic times and the common person of the twentieth century. He knew Jesus in person; I know him by faith. I look forward to that day when we shall be together, comparing notes in the very presence of the Father and the Son and the Holy Spirit.

# Peter

## (FIRST CENTURY)

## BARRETT McGURN

A native of Bethsaida, a village near Lake Tiberias, the son of John (or Jonah), and called Simon, he lived and worked as a fisherman in Capernaum, on Lake Genesareth. His brother Andrew introduced him to Christ, who gave him the name Cephas, the Aramaic equivalent of Peter (the rock). He was present at Christ's first miracle, at Cana, and his home at Capernaum, where Christ cured his mother-in-law, and his boat were always at the Savior's disposal. When he acknowledged Christ as "the Christ . . . the Son of the living God," Jesus replied, "You are Peter and on this rock I will build my Church" (Matt. 16:16–18). It is this statement that underlies Catholic teaching that Peter was the first pope, and the whole concept of the papacy. He is mentioned more frequently in the Gospels than any other of the apostles, was with Christ during many of his miracles, but denied him in the courtyard of Pontius Pilate's palace when Christ was captured.

He appears as the leader of the Christians in Jerusalem after Christ's ascension; he designated Judas' successor, was the first of the apostles to preach to the gentiles and the first *to perform miracles, and preached to and converted many. He was imprisoned by Herod Agrippa about the year 43 but, led by an angel, escaped. He strongly proclaimed at the assembly in Jerusalem that Christ wanted the good news preached to all, affirming Paul's plea that Christianity be preached to all and not only the Jews, but after this reference in Acts 12, except for Acts 15:7–11 there is no further mention of Peter in the New Testament. A very early tradition says he went to Rome, where he was Rome's first bishop, and was crucified about 64, during Nero's reign, at the foot of Vatican Hill. Excavations under St. Peter's unearthed what is believed to be his tomb, and bones found there are still under intensive study. With Paul, his feast day is celebrated on June 29.*

The gospel figure who has always fascinated me in a special way is Peter, the Galilean fisherman who became the Church's foundation rock.

To people of our century Peter is a reassuring personality, no matter how lowly or lofty our position. As the world's population expands, as national governments oversee greater numbers of people, it is easy for anyone to feel rather helpless, to sense that he is out of touch with the centers of power, to believe that little he can do can be of much moment. It was to just that widely felt sentiment that President Jimmy Carter was responding, just after his inauguration, when he invited tens of thousands of fellow citizens to put in telephone calls to him at the White House to share with him their ideas and worries; the President sensed the frustration and sought to alleviate it. And it is to all of us with such reactions that Peter speaks, for who had a better right to perceive himself as inadequate, indeed as clumsy and inept, than the Peter we see in the Gospels? Who had less reason to believe that he could have impact on the affairs of his fellow men, indeed on the very course of Western civilization? Yet the effect of the preaching by Peter's early band has been immeasurable.

Go back to the Gospels if you are unsure of the way Peter is described. Far from the majestic personage you would expect as the first pope, you encounter an awkward, almost comic character. Jesus walks upon the waters; Peter follows suit and nearly drowns. Peter looks on at the Transfiguration and hears God's voice from the clouds; all Peter can think of is to offer tents to Jesus, Moses, and Elijah. Knowing him full well, Christ finds it necessary to advise Peter to say nothing as they descend the mountain: Peter would get things wrong. Peter cannot comprehend the new law of total charity; what does it mean, should one forgive a foe seven times? Not at all, comes the reprimand: seven times seventy! Gethsemane sees the climax. Peter vows to be faithful unto death. At first he is unable even to stay awake. Later he is timorous, even craven, as he swears he never knew Jesus. It is easy for later Christian generations to affirm that they would have done better. In fact the stories of the martyrs and Peter's own later conduct, reported by tradition, suggest that, but who has not shared Peter's weakness on occasion? Whether it be the soldier trembling under the enemy assault or the parent of a family all but overwhelmed by household crises, who is alien to Peter's frailty?

Yet it was this Peter, this "blue-collar worker," this man of no theological pretensions, to whom were given heaven's keys as prince of the apostles. It was he who had to accept the burdens of leadership as the earliest Christians clustered together in Jerusalem and then set off to preach the good news of the new law. To all who despair of what they may do, Peter is a tower of reassurance.

It is not just to the lowliest that Peter's example serves, but also to those in the places of greatest authority, for none of us in an ever-more-complicated world has all the information, wisdom, and strength he would like to possess in order to discharge his responsibilities most effectively. All of us, like Peter, must recognize that we are less than we would wish to be to meet all the challenges and opportunities we encounter. Certainly that has been my own experience.

Peter's story begins in the Gospels but goes on from there. The sharply etched personality of the gospel stories becomes much mistier as we attempt to follow Peter's later course. There has been a strong tradition in Rome, since the second century and perhaps before, that Peter finished his life there, serving as the first pope and then dying with St. Paul on the same day in the seventh decade of the first century. The eloquent, peripatetic Paul is far more visible in the epistles and in the Acts. Romans in these days honor both Peter and Paul jointly on the same great feast day, a major Roman holiday, June 29.

This postgospel Peter especially interested me for many years in Rome. I lived in the Eternal City for half the time from the late thirties to the end of the sixties, going through the underground passages of the catacombs, visiting the endless parade of great churches, and pondering often about those first Christians, of the time of Peter and Paul, wondering what it was like for them in Rome and marveling at the impact they have had on every Western century since then.

If Peter was timorous at Gethsemane, he had ample reasons for terror in Rome. I thought of that often as I walked to work from our home on the Janiculum Hill above St. Peter's Basilica to my office on the city's far side. In America in this century it is hard to conceive of that distant Rome of the first century, togaed Rome. It seems so far in the past as to be almost mythical. Even on your first experience with Rome it is difficult to believe that there was ever a time when it was not Christian. The bells of all the churches fill the air and almost drown out the whine of the *circolare* trolley cars on the curves, or the horns of the minuscule Fiats.

Not a great deal of imagination is needed, however, to recreate the Rome when there were no Christian bell towers, the Rome when the still-standing five-stories-tall Pantheon was what its name still proclaims: the temple of the many pagan gods. That long-surpassed Rome of Augustus and Nero is still tangibly present if one but looks around. Walk down the Aurelian Way toward the center of the city; the aqueduct beside you still brings the Romans their drinking water, as it did when the first Christians arrived from Jerusalem. Go to the lip of the Janiculum Hill with the heart of the city below you, and off to the right is the island in the Tiber. The bridges that carry automobiles there now are the same ones that supported chariots and pedestrians in the time of Peter and the other newly arrived Christians. Across the bridge is the Jewish ghetto. The ghetto's cobbled streets are too narrow and twisty for cars to pass. Often as I walked those streets I mused that the converts from the Holy Land most likely would have sought out fellow Jews on arriving in those first postgospel years. The estrangement between Jew and Christian did not come until the later decades of the first century. The Jewish colony was already well established in Rome in Augustus' time. Did Peter perhaps walk those very streets? I often wondered.

Press on beyond the ghetto toward the seven hills, as I have often done, and other first-century impressions rush in upon you. Just beside the ghetto is the four-story-tall Theater of Pompey. It is now what it was then, an imposing gray stone mass. Now it is a rather sleepy, ancient monument, but in the days of those very first Christians, Peter's time, it was a scene of terror. Romans with a fine civic sense had served their city bravely as soldiers in the legions. They had succeeded all too well, vanquishing all foes, and then they had fallen victim to their own success. Supported by tribute from the colonies, they lived in idleness, sought and exhausted diversions, hunted new thrills, and finally slipped into deep depravity. The story is told of theatrical performances in Pompey's theater in which the jaded audiences were titillated by an extra fillip at the climax of the performances. The actors playing the bad guys would be replaced by condemned prisoners from the prisons. The executions called for by the plot would be carried out in fact with the hapless convicts put to death for the delectation of the bloodthirsty spectators.

Man's inhumanity to man had reached new depths in pagan imperial Rome.

The Rome encountered by that first Christian generation ruled the whole world, exercising an immense influence, which in some ways has endured ever since, but it was also a city of despotism and fear. A mad emperor, murderer of his mother and his wife, and later a suicide, was in power, a threat to everyone. How much Nero was dreaded and despised became clear at his death. The monuments he had erected to himself were torn down, much as I was to see throngs doing to the statues of Stalin in Budapest during the 1956 revolution. It was into that Rome that the Petrine band came with its "good news," the news of the new dispensation, the news of charity and hope as well as of faith, the news of every man's worth, the news of salvation.

Often as I walked Rome's streets I thought of how electric the city's reaction must have been. To some the preachings of a Peter were blasphemy. On the Capitoline Hill was Jupiter's temple. Rome was a theocratic society. To reject Rome's many pagan gods and to affirm Christ was to tamper with the philosophical foundations of the state. The Peter of those years could no longer have been the timid man of Gethsemane. He must have had the courage of lions. For that alone he would deserve the admiration of the later Christian generations.

Where some were outraged, others must have been moved to the depths of their spirits by those first preachers of Christianity in Rome. Walk just outside the Colosseum and you can see the school of the gladiators, a place where men were trained for mortal combat against their fellows. Men had to kill or be killed, often suffering both fates. How deep must have been the despair of those life-death entertainers. The memory must have been vivid of the previous century, when Spartacus at Mount Vesuvius had led a revolt of the gladiators. For a while the troops of Spartacus had held out, fighting their real enemies, the Romans, instead of one another. Then they were vanquished and crucified, one every one hundred feet or so along the Appian Way for as long a distance as that of Naples to Rome. Think what it must have been to such men to hear the message of hope that such as Peter brought.

Tradition says that Peter was crucified upside down near Nero's circus, at the Vatican Hill, and that he was buried just beneath the spot now covered by Michelangelo's famous dome (the model, incidentally, for our own Capitol in Washington). As a newspaper reporter in Rome, I wrote many stories about the search for the historic Peter. Was he indeed interred beneath the papal high altar? Pius XII gave us a running story by having many scores of truckloads of earth carted out from within the sixteen-century-old foundations that were constructed by Constantine. Much circumstantial evidence supporting the ancient tradition was turned up. For instance, it became clear that Constantine, in the first years of the fourth century, had chosen a most unlikely site for the world's greatest Christian church. He had to dig deeply into the side of Vatican Hill on the one side and to level up the ground an equal amount on the other side in order to create the vast ledge on which the basilica still rests. You may note as you go up into St. Peter's that it is a persistent climb all the way. Also, what appeared to the excavators far under the floor of the present church was an ancient cemetery, surely the logical place for the apostle's interment. Be sure to go under the basilica to visit that cemetery on your next Rome trip. You can walk a street of two millennia ago, visiting the mausoleums of pagan families of that dramatic Roman first century.

If so, where is Nero's circus? No one knows. My old professor of physics and seismology from Fordham, Father J. Joseph Lynch, came to Rome at one time to use principles similar to those he employs in the earthquake-detecting center on the Rose Hill campus. He asked me to help. We strung out light explosive charges along a line, set them off, and read the shock waves that went back to Father Lynch's register. His hope was that differing consistencies in the soil beside the big basilica would show us the outlines of the circus, tucked away beneath the many buildings of Vatican City. But we found nothing. That bit of the historic Peter remained elusive.

But, to me, that was not what was important about Peter, the first apostle and the rock of the Church foundation. What was instead of central concern was that those first Christian travelers from the Middle East, blue-collar workers —fishermen or whatever—daringly entered the capital of the ancient world at the risk and cost of life to preach a new faith and philosophy which has influenced Western history, thought, and values ever since. We date the calendar from those days and men. The chivalry of the Middle Ages was their child. The social consciousness a Westerner may take for granted (until he experiences its absence in other parts of the planet) can be traced to the preaching and leadership of Peter in those days of infant Christianity.

During the late sixties on the Janiculum Hill, in Rome, the great basilica of St. Peter was just below our front porch, crowding the view before us. That alone would fill one's mind with Peter. But even elsewhere, wherever you may be in the Eternal City, with the endless procession of the popes (and I had the privilege of meeting each of them through the middle third of this century), Peter, like Paul, can never be far from one's thoughts. Any of these would be reason enough for special devotion to that first apostle, yet all fade in comparison with the real reason. Our whole Western world and life were changed radically by the missionary efforts of Peter and his companions. How fortunate we have been because of them! And what an example Peter is for each of us as we weigh our merits, ponder our potentialities, bend beneath worries and uncertainties, and wonder whether it will ever be possible for us to measure up to the demands made upon us and the opportunities opening before us!

# Paul

## (FIRST CENTURY)

## E. E. Y. HALES

*Born, of Jewish parents descended from the tribe of Benjamin, sometime between 5 and 15 in Tarsus, which made him a citizen of Rome, Saul studied under the famous Rabbi Gamaliel in Jerusalem, became a rigid Pharisee, and was a tentmaker by trade. He was a rabid persecutor of the Christians and was present, though only a spectator, at the stoning of Stephen. On the way to Damascus to arrest some Christians and bring them back to Jerusalem for trial, he experienced his famous encounter with Christ, which led not only to his conversion but, in view of his tremendous impact on early Christianity, was to shape the whole Christian experience. He spent the next three years in Arabia and then returned to Damascus to preach. He immediately encountered fierce opposition from the Jews, which was to continue through the rest of his life and travels. Forced to flee the enmity of the Nabataean king, Aretas, he went to Jerusalem, where through the intercession of Barnabas he met the disciples and, with some opposition, was accepted by the Christian community.*

*He returned to Tarsus for several years but was brought to*

Antioch by Barnabas, was made a teacher in the church there, and after accompanying Barnabas with a donation to the church in Jerusalem, in 44, was sent, with Barnabas, to preach the gospel on the first of his three missionary journeys (45–49), which were to spread Christianity to the gentile world. He went to Cyprus, Perga, Antioch in Pisidia, and the cities of Lycaonia (it was on this journey he changed his name to Paul). On his return, he went to Jerusalem, in about 49, and convinced Peter, James, and the other apostles that gentile Christians need not be circumcised or obliged to accept the Jewish law—a decision with far-reaching effects, since it ensured the universality of Christianity—and secured the approval of his mission to the gentiles. Shortly after his return to Antioch, Paul and Barnabas set out on their second journey. He revisited the churches he had founded on his first journey, crossed to Macedonia (as a result of a dream), thus bringing the gospel to Europe for the first time, and founded churches in Philippi (where he was imprisoned and escaped miraculously), Thessalonica, and Beroea. He preached on the Unknown God in Athens, with little effect, and then spent about two years at Corinth (51–52), where he founded a flourishing church. He then returned to Antioch but soon set off on his third journey (52–56). He spent two years at Ephesus, teaching and working miracles there and in the surrounding area. Driven from Ephesus by a riot of silversmiths, whose trade in statues and shrines to Diana was adversely affected by Christianity, he went to Macedonia and then to Jerusalem with contributions to the mother church. There he was attacked by mobs of Jews for his missions to the gentiles and arrested by the Roman soldiers. When, after two years, he was not tried, he demanded and was granted a trial in Rome as a Roman citizen. On the way to Rome he was shipwrecked off the coast of Malta but eventually reached Rome, where he remained under house arrest for two years (61–63)—the last mention of him in Acts, the major source of biographical information about him. According to Clement of Rome, writing some thirty years after his death, *he was released, went to Spain, and (according to the pastoral epistles) then revisited Ephesus, Macedonia, and Greece. Tradition has him arrested again, probably at Troas, and returned to Rome, where he was beheaded, in 67, during Nero's persecution of the Christians. His feast day with that of Peter is celebrated on June 29.*

It was the electrifying drama of Saint Paul's conversion that thrilled me as a child. The sudden light from heaven as he rode toward Damascus, the voice crying, "Saul, Saul, why are you persecuting me?" the persecutor halted in his tracks, thrown to the ground, blinded, his companions seeing nothing but hearing a voice, a voice that said, "I am Jesus, and you are persecuting me" (Acts 9:4–5).

The Bible is full of dramatic and compelling stories, but I know of none more compelling than this or more persuasive of the truth of the Christian message. If Jesus could intervene in that sort of way, from heaven, on behalf of the Christians, what more was there to be said? But when I grew up I realized, of course, that revelations such as Paul had were not to be expected by ordinary people like myself; you had to be a saint, like Joan of Arc, for that sort of thing. I continued, however, to believe, and still do, that moments of special illumination are granted, just very occasionally, to most of us in the course of our lives, and we do well to heed them when they come. I am glad, for instance, I heeded one that came to me the evening I first met the girl who was to be my wife; and I am glad I heeded one that carried me, at the age of forty, into the Catholic Church.

This latter revelation came to me not as a blinding light from heaven, nor cataclysmically, since it didn't turn my life inside out; I had already been reading and thinking much about religion and was a regular communicant in the Church of England. Yet in its quiet way it was decisive, and in its quiet way it, too, was concerned with light. I was working at the time in Paris, and when a free Saturday afternoon came around I persuaded a Catholic colleague, who was on the same job, to take a walk with me and enlighten me a little on the belief of Catholics. We walked together in the gardens of the Luxembourg Palace without my hearing much that made any particular impression, and from there we walked into the great church of Saint Sulpice, which at that time seemed to me rather formidable and even gloomy, with statues that were austere and reproving and relics that reminded me of the biology laboratory at school. However, during our tour of all this, my colleague slipped away to pray at an altar illumined by a forest of candles, an occurrence that impressed me a good deal, unaccustomed as I then was to the use of churches as places for private prayer or devotion. And more impressive still, in fact for me no less than an illumination, was to hear my colleague say, quite casually, as we left the church together, "I have put up a very large candle for you!"

A born Catholic will find it hard to understand why so simple and obvious an act should have impressed me so much; in fact, now that the first fine careless rapture of conversion has faded, as all things fade, I myself find it rather hard to understand. But I know what it was (humanly speaking) that hit me: it was the simplicity of an implicit faith and the concern for my soul that that candle implied. On our walk my colleague had made no great effort to argue or explain (though very well qualified to do both) but in the church there were this prayer and a very big candle—acts, not arguments. All the tedious apologetics I had read and found only half convincing, the arguments about the Petrine texts, the apostolic succession, or the infallibility of the Church, went for little by comparison, and so, I am sorry to say, did the 370 propositions of the penny catechism that I bought on my return to England.

It must have been some three years later that the priest who had received me into the Church said it was time I was confirmed, and what saint's name would I choose? Another shock (life is full of shocks for the convert). "Paul," I said, remembering the story of that great light from heaven and then that candle that had burned in Saint Sulpice.

But I was still singularly ignorant of the real Paul and of his overwhelming significance. Though I was a historian by avocation, my field of study lay in the nineteenth century; such knowledge as I had of earlier events lay buried with my Oxford past and had never included much about Paul. Only quite a lot later did I come to understand that Paul was not only a saint with a strong magnetic pull, a wonderful ear for a phrase, and unlimited courage and endurance, but historically speaking undoubtedly the saint of saints, the cornerstone in the arch of Christianity. From a small sect of dissident Jews, still mainly concerned to demonstrate that Christ was the long-awaited Messiah, he had raised the sights of the early Church to embrace the known world, proclaiming what theologians call the Christ-Event, by which they mean the redemption of the world by the incarnation, crucifixion, and resurrection of Our Lord. This, Paul insisted, was in itself and of itself nothing less than the offer of salvation to the whole of mankind, the rebirth of the human race. That was how he understood the life and death and resurrection of Christ, so that his mission to the Gentiles was no mere extension of the good news from the Jews to other, neighbouring races, or later to Rome, astonishing as that achievement was; it meant the inclusion of the totality of mankind in this cataclysmic event if only they were willing to receive it—and even, in a sense, if they weren't.

Humanly speaking, it is hard to see historically how Christianity could have conquered the known world, as it did, without the work of Paul. How would it ever have disengaged itself from Judaic law and custom, seeing how cautious even the boldest of the apostles, Peter, was when compelled to face the issue of accepting other customs and traditions? If Christianity was to win recognition as the true religion for all mankind, it required the dynamic of no less a person than Paul, that dynamic imparted to him by his conversion and his unique vision of the nature of the sacrifice of Christ, a

Christ who was the Messiah, yes, but so much more than the Messiah awaited by the Jews.

To his total absorption by his unprecedented message we must attribute Paul's fortitude and perseverance in affliction, those sufferings we all know about because we hear them in church in his second letter to the wayward and fickle men of Corinth: "Five times the Jews scourged me, and spared me but one lash in the forty; three times I was beaten with rods; once I was stoned; I have been shipwrecked three times, I have spent a night and a day as a castaway at sea. What journeys I have undertaken, in danger from rivers, in danger from robbers, in danger from my own people, in danger from the gentiles; danger in cities, danger in the wilderness, danger in the sea, danger among false brethren!"* So much violence and so much danger, besides the weariness, the hunger, and the cold (and how about the heat?) inseparable from those missionary journeys he undertook through the countries of the eastern Mediterranean, and on that final journey to Nero's Rome, where he was imprisoned and suffered, in the end, his martyrdom. What but the extraordinary nature of the message he had to convey could have enabled him to surmount all this, even glorying that he was accounted worthy so to suffer, worthy to help make up—it is his own odd phrase —what was lacking in the sufferings of Christ?

I think if I had known, at the time of my conversion, what I now know about Paul, I would have shrunk from suggesting my name be linked with his at my confirmation. The names I had been given by my parents were three good English names, all belonging to my family, but only one of them, Edward, was a saint's name, and even he only a semidouble in the Roman Missal and little known outside England. To have added to my names the name of Paul would have seemed to me like having very potent wine added to my earthly vessels. Of course, I would have been wrong. I now realize we need all the help we can get, the more potent the

---

* 2 Cor. 11:24–26 (Knox translation).

better. But born Catholics should remember that those who come from outside arrive quite unprepared for the easy and familiar terms on which those within live and converse with exalted saints, saints who enjoy doubles of the first class and every sort of dignity but whom they are ready enough to reprove when things go wrong. I needn't have felt any embarrassment when I asked to be called Paul, and I'm glad I made bold to do so.

He is my favorite saint in the sense that I admire most what he did and think it was of the greatest importance; but if I had the chance of a few days in the company of one of the great saints I might well choose somebody else: Saint Augustine, for instance, or Saint Thomas More. Paul's human personality, which appeals so strongly to many, I would have found, I think, a little overwhelming. He must have been a man of extraordinary physical stamina, probably one of those wiry men who have such resilience; we know how energetic he was even in his persecuting days. He should be accounted the natural patron of all those who love pioneering adventure, of the hikers who have not been slow to follow in his footsteps along the coast of Syria to Antioch and on into Pamphylia, Lydia, and Macedonia, standing, in their shorts, as their grandfathers once stood in knickerbockers, on the "very spot" at Ephesus or Corinth or Athens where Paul once stood and preached—muscular Christians, honoring with muscular endeavor their tireless hero. Nature has not fitted me to be one of those, to honor Paul thus in my body. But there is much, too, for the mere sedentary scholar to like about Paul on the human level. I like his indignations, and I like especially that frank confession about a sting in his flesh—what sting?—which he welcomes because it prevents his thinking too well of himself. And I like the touch of vanity that makes him recount, surely with relish, how he had to be let down from the city wall at Damascus in a basket or how he stood up to Peter and got away with it. He is never really boasting, because he makes it so clear that anything he has achieved has been only by the grace of God, and that to talk about such things is only foolishness, but he is prepared to do it just the same; he is not going to let anybody think that other leaders of the early Church had anything on him in what they were prepared to undergo. Most of all, I like—still on the human plane—the well-known story of his encounter with the learned men of Athens, the way he teased them for setting up an altar "to an Unknown God," and the way they teased him back, saying, "We'll listen to you on this topic some other time"—surely one of the most amusing stories in Holy Scripture.

But, as I say, there are other saints with whom, on the human level, I feel more personal affinity and with whom I could probably have talked with less personal embarrassment. The point about Paul is simply that he is the saint to whom I feel that as Christians we owe most—the indispensable saint without whose labors it is impossible to visualize the emergence of the Church as we understand her. One feels—I hope this is not heretical—that Our Lord called Paul into His service, at a very sticky time, because the immense task of laying the foundations of the One Church, universal and all-sufficing, simply wasn't going to get done if He didn't; so when I say he is my favorite saint it is less a matter of personal empathy than of overwhelming gratitude. We stand enormously in his debt today and on every other day that has been or is yet to come.

This being so, it is odd that in some ways we seem to esteem him less than we used. He still enjoys, of course, a unique attention in our liturgy and something like parity of official esteem with Peter himself; but I don't think that, in popular esteem, he is an "in" saint in quite the way he was. In some ways this may be a good thing; for instance we may be thankful ours is not the enthusiasm of the eighteen thirties, which made of Paul, because he said the Old Law was superseded, the idol of every wild and extreme sect, so that "Pauline" churches in New England and New York taught we should despise the Law and live only for the love of God —alas, it soon became for human loves. We may also perhaps be glad that less attention is paid today to some of the things he said about the authority of husbands and fathers or the subordination of women; there is room for two views about his attitude, which was the prevailing one in his own day; but certainly his teaching is out of harmony with our current ideas of freedom and equality.

More importantly, we tend, I think, to miss the unique importance of Paul today because we are no longer historically minded, at least in matters of religion, and you need to be historically minded to appreciate the significance of Paul. For he was, quite simply, after Our Lord, the architect of the Christian Church. We assume, vaguely, that because of its divine origin or because "the truth will ultimately prevail," Christianity was bound to establish itself till the whole earth was filled with the glory of it. But it wasn't. Our Lord guaranteed His Church against error; He didn't guarantee what the gathered harvest would amount to. That, He warned, would depend on the soil, which might be shallow and stony, and on the laborers, who, He knew, were few and faint of heart. As a plain matter of historical fact it is to the vision and labors of Paul that we owe the Church as we understand her, the Church available equally to all men and women everywhere, bringing salvation to gentile and to Jew, to white and to black, to fathers and mothers and children and slaves and heroes and cowards and clever men like the men of Athens, and silly men like those around the Prince Regent at Brighton, England, and rich men on Wall Street, and poor people, very, very poor, in Sicily and Naples, and lazy people, who follow the sun from sandy beach to sandy beach. All one in the body of Christ, all equally His concern, all equally inseparable from His love.

# Augustine

## (354–430)

### ANNE FREMANTLE

Born on November 13 at Tagaste, North Africa, son of Patricius, a pagan Roman official, and Monica, a Christian, he received a Christian upbringing and in 370 went to Carthage to study at the university. He studied law but gave it up to devote himself to literary pursuits, and gradually abandoned his Christian faith, taking a mistress with whom he lived for fifteen years and who bore him a son, Adeodatus. He became interested in philosophy, and about 373 embraced Manichaeism. After teaching at Tagaste and Carthage for the next decade, he went to Rome and opened a school there but became discouraged with the attitude of his students, and in 384 accepted the chair of rhetoric at Milan. There, impressed by the sermons of Ambrose, bishop of Milan, and his tutor Simplicianus, he became a Christian. With his mother, brother, and several others, he lived a community life of prayer and meditation. In 387 he started back to Africa, and on the way Monica died, at Ostia. The following year, he founded a monastery at Tagaste. His son died in 389, and Augustine was ordained in 391 and established a religious community. Despite his monastic life, he began *preaching and met with phenomenal success. He was made coadjutor to Bishop Valerius of Hippo in 395 and succeeded to the see on Valerius' death, the following year. He became the outstanding figure in African church affairs and was the leader in bitter fights against Manichaeism, the Donatists, and the Pelagians. He died in Hippo, during Genseric's siege of that city, on August 28. Augustine's towering intellect molded the thought of Western Christianity to such an extent that his philosophy and theology dominated the Western world for a thousand years after his death. He wrote profusely defending and expositing the faith, and to this day many of his works are of major importance in philosophy and theology. Among his best-known works are his* Confessions *(one of the great spiritual classics of all times),* City of God, *and* The Trinity. *Called Doctor of Grace, he was the greatest of the fathers and doctors of the Church and, with the possible exception of Thomas Aquinas, the greatest single intellect the Catholic Church has ever produced.*

What does one look for in a "favorite" saint? Above all, two things, I think: that one should be drawn to him as a person and that he should, as the Quakers put it, "speak to my condition." That is, the same sort of reciprocity one seeks in any friendship, a reciprocity of affection, since that is the only one that can exist between a sinner still here on earth and a saint safely in heaven.

I was in my early teens when I first met Augustine. My father died when I was twelve, leaving my mother badly off, with two young girls to educate (my sister was ten) and a house in Savoy, France, where I had been born, which my father had left her. She decided to move there, and there we remained for two blissful years. Our education was taken care of by a fat French lady who came daily and by Latin lessons twice a week with the village curé, l'Abbé Premillieu, son of Savoyard peasants but very well educated. Once a week he came to us; once a week we went to him. I adored Latin, reveling in Virgil, detesting Caesar, doting on Seneca. How great these pagan writers were! What had the Christians done but made the world "grow with their breath" (Mama had known Swinburne and loved his poetry). M. le Curé was shocked at my attitude and offered Augustine as an antidote. I fell, of course, at once: here was a writer as superb as any pagan but with such a marvelous passion in his language, so much better than those chilly Romans concerned with how to dress their vines and how pious Aeneas escaped from Troy. And the cry of Augustine "*Sero Te amavi, pulchritudo tam antiqua et tam nova, sero Te amavi*" ("Late have I loved Thee, beauty so ancient and so new, late have I loved Thee") still gives me the same shiver of delight as when I first heard it. Indeed, everything he wrote is so well written! St. Jerome was scolded by God (in a dream) for being "more of a Ciceronian than a Christian": I fear at thirteen I became an Augustinian and, only with Augustine's help, have subsequently tried to become a Christian.

Augustine came of Berber stock, and so was black, but not a Negro. He was not baptized at birth—no one was in those days, because to sin after baptism was considered much worse than to do so before, so everyone put baptism off to the last possible moment, even Christians as public in their conversion as the Emperor Constantine, who was baptized only on his deathbed, though he had openly proclaimed his faith after winning the battle of the Milvian bridge. Augustine remembers being suckled, and being jealous of his younger brother, who was being suckled too; he was the most normal of small boys, loving to play, loathing school, preferring to rob his neighbor's pear tree than to gather the fruit from his own, and wailing to his parents when he was beaten by his teacher. His parents only laughed at him, and, remembering he had heard his mother and the servants speak of a powerful Being who watches over orphans and unhappy children, he prayed, "Dear God, may I not be beaten at school." But God was as hard-hearted as his parents. Augustine was desperate, and, forty years later, so well remembered his misery as to make his readers feel it too. But though he hated school, he was very bright, and his parents decided to send him to Madaura, an old Numidian city about thirty miles from Tagaste, where he studied Greek, which he never really mastered and which bored him, and Virgil, whom he loved so much that until the end of his life he would quote him: always, the story of Dido moved him to tears.

But, above all, he loved the African light. He described often the luminous countryside, the great buildings, Numidian and Roman, saturated with sun, and the colors of sunset and sunrise irradiating the landscape of the great plains that ended in desert. He boarded with a pagan friend of his father's, and the culture he absorbed was all pre-Christian, in very much the same way as a brilliant adolescent today, studying in New York, would absorb a post-Christian culture. And how Augustine loved *things*, writing later, "If sensible objects had no soul, one would not love them so much." Light, landscape, color, shapes—he loved them, as shortly he would love his friends. And then, shortly after puberty, he went on to Carthage, one of the five great capitals of the Roman Empire: Rome, Antioch, Alexandria, Constantinople, and Carthage.

Here, he declared, he wasn't yet in love, but he wanted to love, and loved, indeed, the very idea of loving. And how he wept at the theater, moved by the plays of two Africans, Terence and Menander, and enjoying every minute of the big-city life: his stay there was paid for by a rich friend of his father's, Romanianus, who went on paying for him when Augustine's father died. Augustine now discovered physical love: he was tender, ready to give himself, but soon discovered that one never gives oneself completely and that, most of the time, this tenderness met with no response. There is always, says the French proverb, one who kisses and one who simply waits to be kissed, and how rare is real reciprocity! He was disappointed each time, and his burning love burnt itself out in brief affairs. Yet he found he needed sex, and settled down to what he calls "voluptuous habits," which did not prevent his getting on with his studies. For basically he was a good bourgeois; especially since his father's death, he knew his mother, younger brother, and sister depended on him: he must do well, must get a good job.

And he found his friendships at least as fulfilling as his loves: Alypius, a childhood friend from Tagaste who was to remain his friend all his life; Nebridius, another dear friend, who died young; and Honoratus, whom he later led with him into Manichaeism, then finally rescued. "What attached me most to my friends," he wrote later, "was the pleasure of talking and laughing with them, to read with them the same books, to joke and talk nonsense, sometimes to argue, but without anger, and thus to emphasize the pleasure of generally agreeing; to miss an absent friend, to welcome his return. We loved each other with all our hearts, and these friendships were expressed by our eyes, our gestures, our voices." He was only once in his life to be so happy again, at Cassiacum, during the first months after his conversion, and before his baptism. At Carthage he really had everything pagan life had to offer: friends, girl-friends, a lovely city to live in, interesting studies to pursue. And then he read a book, one that he read only because it was required for a course, a book that has since completely disappeared, the *Hortensius*, of Cicero.

Augustine was nineteen when, suddenly, this book made his heart beat faster, and a marvelous vision flooded his soul, which leaped as a result of what he read. What was in this lost book? Augustine tells us it contained a panegyric to wisdom, and he quotes the following words, which occurred at the end of a long discussion: "If, as the ancient philosophies pretend (and they are the greatest and most famous), we have a divine and immortal soul, we must believe that the longer it has followed the path of wisdom, that is to say, that it has pursued reason, the love of learning and of truth, the less it will be caught and soiled by human passions and errors, and the easier it will be for it to rise and return to heaven." These words made Augustine despise the rhetoric he was studying, the honors and glory he was seeking. What were they, in comparison with wisdom? He felt ready to abandon them all in order to pursue wisdom only. These uplifting reflections made him wonder if there might not be something in the Christian teachings. Did they, too, promise wisdom? So he set himself to read the Bible, but found it harsh and crude: this direct, popular style, which cared not at all how things were said, put him off: whatever faith he had had as a child he had lost when his senses woke: "Reading [the Bible] I found the threshold too low, and did not wish to bow my head to enter." So he gave up, and soon after joined the Manichaeans as an auditor.

Who were the Manichaeans? Mani, their founder, was born A.D. 215, in the village of Mardinu, Babylonia. His father joined a sect, the Moghtasilah, whose followers abstained from flesh, wine, and women. At thirteen, Mani had his first revelation, at twenty-five a more urgent one. At twenty-seven he preached at the court of the Persian King Shapur I, whose brother first favored Mani then returned to his original Mazdaism (Zoroastrianism) and exiled Mani, who wandered to India, Turkestan, Tibet, and China, where Manichaeans continued to be found until the thirteenth century. Mani returned to Persia in 273, under a new king, Bahram I. But, two years later, in March 275, Mani was seized, flayed alive, and beheaded; his skin was stuffed with straw and hung up in public. What did Mani teach? the irreconcilable duality of the Light and Darkness, which did not even predicate a final victory for the Light, as Zoroaster and the later Gnostics had done.

The two elements, light and darkness, are found in all things, animate and inanimate, and the Manichaean's duty is to free the elements of light in himself and in all things. The Manichaeans believed that not only darkness but also light was material—everything was material, some things made of fine matter, others of coarse: God Himself is made of the finest matter, sparks of which are present in us and there strive to cast off the bonds of the darkness also present in us. Augustine felt in his own nature the truth of Manichaeism: he was aware of the struggle between light and darkness in himself. Manichaeism held that one was not responsible for the evil he does: it is the work of the Dark Principle, who "works in us" to commit sins. Augustine, who just at this time was settling down with the nameless woman with whom he lived and to whom he was faithful for fourteen years, by whom he had his only child, Adeodatus, found the Manichaean doctrine convenient.

His mother did not. Monica was so horrified at the change in her son—he returned to Tagaste in 374 with a job, teaching grammar—that she would not allow him to stay at home, and he was obliged to board with Romanianus. This did not make him think better of Christians and their charity; in fact, he converted Romanianus, Alypius, Honoratus, and others to Manichaeism, and later confessed to Christ, "I did even bay against Thee!" (He also took to drawing horoscopes.) He had plenty of students, as Romanianus was the greatest patron in Tagaste, and everyone wanted to take lessons from the brilliant young man of twenty living in his house.

My mother claimed to be a Manichaean. She refused to believe God made earwigs (insects she much disliked) and thought the Manichaean premise of two equal powers, of darkness and light, got one out of the difficulty Fyodor Dostoevsky set out so marvelously in *The Brothers Karamazov*: how God could be good and let innocent children suffer. Rather than "very respectfully give back her ticket" to such a God (as Ivan Karamazov declared he had done), she preferred to believe God guiltless, the Devil guilty. I found Augustine's nine-year spiritual sojourn with the Manichaeans comforting, as it proved how seriously he took the problem of evil. I was a child in World War I, and that ghastly holocaust—twenty thousand men killed in a day in the "trench-abattoirs of Passchendaele," over one million English alone in the four years, and as many French, Germans, etc., all for what?—was the climate of my nursery. We could hear the guns in France from our Sussex garden.

Augustine's Christian solution of the problem of evil was a very orthodox one: that nothing is evil, only the use we make of it can be evil, and so often is. Thus, whatever is, is good, as he wrote in the *Confessions*. "So therefore as long as things are, they are good: therefore whatsoever is, is good. The evil then which I sought, whence it is, is not any substance, for were it a substance, it should be good. . . . I perceived therefore, and it was manifested to me, that Thou madest all things good, nor is there any substance at all which Thou madest not. . . . And to Thee is nothing whatsoever evil: yea, not only to Thee, but also to Thy creation as a whole, because there is nothing without, which may break in and corrupt that order which Thou hast appointed. And I perceived and found it nothing strange that bread which is pleasant to a healthy palate is loathsome to one distempered, and to sore eyes light is offensive, which to the sound eye is delightful. And Thy righteousness displeaseth the wicked. . . . And I enquired what iniquity was and found it to be no substance, but the perversion of the will turned aside from Thee."

So even our sins are the bad use of God-given good: avarice, of the hoarding of what we should share; greed, the excess of what is needed for life (food); in the sins of the flesh, the pleasure is good, only the person by whom we procure the pleasure can be an error of choice. But what of the suffering of children? When it is not caused by our own mishandling of them, by our lack of knowledge of how to help, we must accept, Augustine insists, that the Creator knows more, and understands more, of any child's suffering—even our own child's—than we do ourselves. It is impossible, Augustine insisted, that the Love that created us could love less than we do.

After Augustine's own conversion, which he movingly described in the *Confessions*, and after the death of Monica, he returned to Africa, never to leave it again. And there his son, Adeodatus, who was only seventeen, died. A brilliant young man, he and his father had collaborated on the book *De*

*Magistro* (*Of the Teacher*), and as Augustine told God, "Thou knowest well that all the thoughts I put into his mouth were his own, and he was but seventeen." This book declares that every soul has a transcendent teacher, for every soul has Christ within itself and questions Him, and "It is He, whether I speak or am spoken to, Who implants the same truth in the mind of him who speaks and him who listens. For there is but one Master, God." Augustine wrote that his son's genius "did almost frighten me," but God cut short his life in this world, and thereafter "his memory is to me more safe."

It is Augustine the mystic whom I love above all. Even more than the writer. Some of his phrases, he put into God's mouth, and they are quite supremely moving. "I am the Food of the Strong," he makes Christ say; "grow, and you shall feed on Me; but in truth it is not I who will turn into you, but you who will be changed into Me." And again, "God did not say, go to the east to find wisdom, sail to the west to find justice: there where you seek, there you shall find, for to Him who is everywhere present, one comes by love and not by sail."

But of all the things he wrote, the thousands of words, the dozens of books, four words seem to me the most important words ever written outside of Holy Writ: *Virtus est ordo amoris.* Virtue is the setting in order of love. This bears out his whole idea of evil as dis-order and of good as the expression of the divine order.

How right he is: if one reads history—and I am an historian by trade—one sees how every time things go wrong it is because of disordered love, whether that love be of country, class, person, or even God. For as the great saints have always noted, the "right ordering" of our loves must begin with the First Commandment. We must love God first and above all, but we must not love Him from any hope of heaven or fear of hell, nor because "who love Thee not are lost eternally," as Francis Xavier's lovely hymn has it. We must love because we are made for, and by, that Love, and it is the highest or-

dering of our life to love the Love that loved us into existence. Little wonder Augustine is for me the best-loved saint—
and it doesn't hurt that I would have loved to meet him,
even to listen to his sermons!

What has Augustine to say to us today? In 1956, shortly
before he died, I gave Dr. Albert Einstein my *Age of Belief*
paperback, with Augustine's passages on time marked, and he
wrote, both in scribbles in German in the book and in a letter to me, how much Augustine's ideas had interested him.
In 1977, one of the Ph.D.s given by Oxford University to a
Balliol College student was for "Problems of self-love in St.
Augustine." But these are academics, high-brows. What good
is Augustine to *l'homme moyen sensuel*, to the average (sen-
sual) man and woman? He is, above all, the saint who perhaps
most of any one of them enjoyed *everything*. Théophile Gau-
tier, the French Romantic poet, once wrote, "I am one for
whom the visible world exists," and as a corrective—or perhaps a correlative—to the present-day enthusiasm of so many
young people for Eastern mysticism, with its emphasis on
maya, on the unreality or the meaninglessness of the world of
the senses, Augustine celebrated, in all his works, the beauty
and the reality of creation reflecting its Creator. For him, the
journey was not away from but through and with the creation, which was wholly good and beautiful; not the flight, as
Plotinus put it, from the unknown to the unknown but from
the loved to the Beloved, a voyage inward indeed but, above
all, upward.

# Patrick—Missionary for Tomorrow

## (c. 389–c. 461)

### Gary MacEoin

*So much of Patrick's life is enshrouded in mists and legends that much of his biography must be conjecture. The son of a Roman-British official, Calpurnius, he was born in a village called Bannavem, probably in Britain but possibly in Gaul. He was captured by raiders when he was about sixteen and carried off to slavery in pagan Ireland. After herding sheep for six years, probably in Antrim or Mayo, he escaped, probably to Gaul. He seems to have studied at the monastery of Lérins, off the coast of France, in 412–15 and then to have gone to Auxerre, where he spent the next fifteen years and was probably ordained there in 417. Probably about 432 he was consecrated bishop by St. Germanus and sent to Ireland to succeed Bishop Palladius, who had died the previous year. He traveled the length and breadth of Ireland, meeting fierce opposition from hostile Druids, whom he reputedly defeated by miraculous means, and chieftains. He eventually converted the island to a Christianity so strong in the faith that it has endured to the present day despite every attempt to eradicate*

*it. He visited Rome about 442, and in 444 founded the ca-*
*thedral of Armagh, which soon became the center of the*
*Church's activities in Ireland.*

*During his three decades in Ireland, he raised the standard*
*of scholarship, encouraged the study of Latin, brought Ire-*
*land into closer relations with the rest of the Western*
*Church, and of course converted the Irish to the faith they*
*have so fiercely defended through the centuries. He wrote*
*Confessio, a self-defense and testament of his activities, the*
*chief source of biographical information about him, and a*
*Letter to the Soldiers of Coroticus, denouncing the slaughter*
*by Coroticus' raiding Welshmen, who were Christians, of a*
*group of Irish Christians. His cult began with his death, on*
*March 17, and has flourished ever since.*

Like everyone else who grew up in a Catholic environment
on either side of the North Atlantic between the First and
Second World Wars, I accepted as an unquestioned fact that
ours was the greatest period of missionary expansion in the
Church's history. Perhaps an occasional person with a flair
for history would suggest a comparable enthusiasm at the
time of the apostles or recall Francis Xavier in the Orient
and the Spanish and Portuguese missionaries who implanted
the faith in South and Central America and north into Mexico and what is now the Southwest of the United States. Yet
even such would agree that no previous period could parallel
the massive involvement in so many countries, the centrally
planned strategy through the Vatican's Congregation for the
Propagation of the Faith, the flood of vocations of men and
women, and the grass-roots support in nickels and dimes,
pennies, francs, guilders, and lire.

And like everyone else whose Catholic environment was
rural Ireland, I was similarly convinced that the quintes-
sential mission spirit was that of the Irish, a people who held
the faith in its purest form and carried it in that same form
around the world. We further took it for granted that the

missionary success of the Irish stemmed from the fact that we have preserved the faith through the centuries in the precise forms in which Saint Patrick brought it to us, and that the techniques of preaching and spreading the faith our missionaries practiced around the world accurately mirrored those Patrick himself used when—as he describes in his autobiographical *Confessio*—he responded to the voice of the Irish calling him in his sleep to come and walk again among them.

This consensus certainly did say something significant about the reverence of the Irish for their patron saint, and nothing occurred to cause me to re-evaluate it or question its historical validity until my fortunes led me to New York, some years after the end of World War II. The previous five years, I had spent in the Caribbean and South America; and the general recession in the United States before we became involved in war in Korea was accentuated for the newspaper industry by the rapid rise of television. After a fruitless search for editorial work on English-language newspapers, I accepted with alacrity an offer to edit the Sunday edition of a Spanish-language daily whose readers were mostly Puerto Ricans. Meanwhile I found an apartment on the upper West Side of Manhattan in a parish in which those who attended Sunday Mass and other functions were overwhelmingly Americans of Irish ancestry. They were served by priests of identical background and outlook, dedicated men who faithfully carried on the traditions of organization, devotions, administration of the sacraments, and forms of worship they had learned in Ireland or from Irish mentors.

My work demanded a knowledge of the location and lifestyle of the more than half a million Puerto Ricans then living in various decayed or decaying sectors of Manhattan, the Bronx, and Brooklyn. To my astonishment, I soon determined that more than half the Catholics in my parish were Puerto Ricans, yet one never saw more than three or four at any service in my parish church. Further investigation established that my parish was typical in this respect.

Yet the Puerto Ricans, as I studied their life-style, revealed themselves as deeply religious. The "storefront" churches springing up on almost every block, with a minimum of theology and a maximum of worshiper involvement, were thronged not only on Sundays but often during the week. Their converts quickly developed a new set of values. They visited the sick in hospital, shared with their neighbors in need. The men stopped drinking to excess and gave up their promiscuous practices.

The explanations offered by various New York priests failed to convince me. "They know their duty," the standard reply ran, with a stress on the *they*. "The doors of our churches are always open and entry is free. If they don't come, they have only themselves to blame."

Then I met a young priest recently arrived in New York from his homeland in East-Central Europe. Shocked to find half a million Catholics ignored by the church authorities and rapidly losing all relationship with their traditional faith, he was searching for reasons and remedies. His name was Ivan Illich, and we met because a Spanish-language newspaper was a logical medium of communication with this group. Materials he gave me included a copy of a study he had drafted with the title of "Missionary Poverty." As far as I know, he never published this paper, but it already contained in embryo the challenging critiques of our assumptions and conventions that have since brought him world fame.

Reading it immediately recalled to me the example of Saint Patrick and sent me back to restudy works I had read often before without discovering in them the significance brought out for me by one whose multifaceted learning I am sure did not include any knowledge of Patrick's missionary practice.

A vast medieval literature, some surviving in writing and more in oral tradition, underlies the popular image of Patrick as one who fought the Druids and magicians of pagan Ireland with their own weapons, vanquishing them with miracles and at times with trickery and violence hardly appropriate to his Christian message. But Patrick in fact left two short writings, autobiographical in nature, that present a radically different picture, one that takes on a highly significant and still-pertinent meaning when read in conjunction with Illich's intellectual evaluation of missionary poverty.

To bring Christ to people of a different culture, Illich argued, the missionary must divest himself of his natural identification with his own culture, particularly if he has been conditioned—as is normal—to regard his own culture as superior to that of the people to whom Christ has sent him. To start, he should immerse himself in the language, achieving an ability to use it effectively as a communication tool while simultaneously acquiring a literary knowledge no less than the level of knowledge he has of the literature of his own culture. In addition, he must immerse himself in the life of his new community until he can think, feel, share the emotions, and suffer the anxieties of its members. Only then can he present Christ in words and symbols that convey his intention and truly incarnate Christ for his hearers. Only then can he begin to differentiate between the essence of the Christian message and the clothing in which he has unconsciously wrapped it.

Since Vatican Council II (1962–65), this has become the established missionary teaching of the Church, even if only a small minority of missionaries have as yet internalized to a significant extent and implemented that teaching. But in the early 1950s it was a challenge to everything that had been institutionalized for at least a century, an institutionalization that derived logically from Rome's condemnation of the Chinese rites in the early-eighteenth century. Throughout the entire colonial era, the missionary in Africa and Asia saw his function as one of "civilizing" people. As a preparation for the acceptance of the Christian message, he had first to introduce them to the manners, customs, dress, and values—and as far as possible also to one of the languages—of Europe or North America. Several generations of "Europeanization" were in practice considered required for elevation to a bishopric or similar position of authority. In Latin America, although the hemisphere had been in principle Catholic for centuries, the same attitude prevailed almost universally.

That was not Patrick's way, as I realized when I reread his two surviving writings, the *Confessio* and the *Letter to the Soldiers of Coroticus*. The former is the longer work, some six thousand words; the latter, fewer than two thousand. Both shed light on Patrick's missionary techniques, but it is the brief *Letter* that is decisive. The *Confessio* is a rapid account of his life and work, written in response to charges from unidentified enemies that Patrick was motivated by pride or a desire for self-aggrandizement in his mission to Ireland. On the contrary, he insists, he has gained nothing in material terms and instead has given up much in order to carry out the task entrusted to him by the Lord.

"This is my confession before I die" are its closing words. It has all the marks of the last message of one aware of how much he has achieved and how little his achievements were his own work. The biographical flashes and glimpses are interwoven with Scripture quotations stressing the inadequacy of the instrument and the wisdom and power with which God's hand had used it. He even finds it necessary to apologize for his poor Latin, the language in which he wrote, because the intended recipients lived across the sea and could not communicate with him in the Gaelic that was now his natural medium of expression. The vicissitudes of his life, the fact that he had spent his youth as a slave in Ireland and had consequently never had the opportunity to learn Latin fluently and achieve the conciseness of expression characteristic of the polished Latinist—all this he notes as evidence of how inadequately he was prepared for his task. But in historical retrospect, what he saw as limitations may be seen as key benefits. If those youthful years during which he was immersed in the language and ways of thinking of the Irish had been spent in a monastic school in Britain or on the Continent, his missionary approach would inevitably have been different, and in all likelihood less successful.

Patrick was himself very clear about the extent of the

sacrifices he had seen as necessary to fulfill his missionary vocation. First of all, he points out, he gave up his "free birth" for the sake of the Irish. He was a Roman citizen, the grandson of a priest and the son of a deacon who was also an official of the Roman provincial government in Britain. By voluntarily leaving the Roman province to reside among the "barbarians," as all living beyond the confines of the empire were regarded by the Romans, he gave up his claim to protection as a free-born Roman. In modern terminology, he relinquished his citizenship in favor of that of his adopted home.

Nor was it easy for him, Patrick concedes, to choose life among strangers, especially among people on whom as a Roman he looked down as uncivilized savages, a people who in addition had grievously wronged him by carrying him as a youth into slavery. To visit my homeland and parents in Britain, and also to get to Gaul to see my brothers, he writes in the *Confessio*, "God knows how deeply I desired. But bound by the Spirit, who warns me that should I do this he would point me out as guilty in the future, I fear to lose the benefit of the work I have begun."

Such is his commitment to his adopted people that "It is there I wish to dwell until I die." And in all of this he never sought personal benefit. "They would take some of their ornaments and lay them on the altar, but I would immediately return them, even though it offended them when I did so." He accepted no money for "so many thousands of people" he baptized or for other services he performed.

One passage in the *Confessio* captures perfectly the impact the Irish made on Patrick and explains how he found it in his heart to become one of them. He had just described how he had been carried into slavery in Ireland, spent six years tending sheep in woods and on mountainsides, escaped to France, and finally returned to his home in Britain, to be received as a son and urged never to leave again. But one night he had a dream. "I saw a man who seemed to be coming from Ireland. His name was Victorinus, and he was carrying an enormous

number of letters. One of these he handed me, and I saw
that it was headed 'The Voice of the Irish.' And as I began
to read, I thought I could hear within me that same voice of
the people who lived near the wood of Foclut, not far from
the Western Sea. And they called out as follows: 'We be-
seech you, holy youth, to come and walk once more among
us.' I was so affected to the depths of my heart that I was unable to read further, and I awakened from my sleep. Thanks
be to God, because many years later he granted them what
they had asked."

The full import of this simple recitation by Patrick of his
way of life and his relationship to the people of Ireland
emerges from a study of the *Letter to the Soldiers of Coroticus*. (Its full title is *Letter to the Christian Subjects of the
Tyrant Coroticus*.) Written late in Patrick's life, the *Letter* is
an impassioned denunciation of a British chieftain named
Coroticus who had raided the Irish coast, killed a number of
Patrick's converts, and carried others off to sell as slaves and
concubines. From start to finish, this document expresses the
total identification of Patrick with the "barbarians" to whom
he had dedicated his life "for the love of God." He is particularly incensed that some of the Christian soldiers of Coroticus seem to think lightly of what they had done, as though
they did not believe that "we have received one baptism or
have one God as father." And then follows his forthright as-
sertion of where he stands: "They think it shameful that we
are natives of Ireland." He rejects both his British and his
Roman birthrights to proclaim himself one of the people who
had grievously wronged him as a youth but had subsequently
more than compensated for that wrong by accepting the message of Christ that the Spirit had commanded him to preach.

Patrick's identification with the Irish was not merely personal. It was expressed even more significantly in the church
structures he created. Whether the conversion of the entire
people of Ireland to Christianity was his exclusive work, or
whether indeed the whole island was converted in his lifetime, can legitimately be questioned. But there is no reason

to doubt his own statements. "I am very much God's debtor," he writes in the *Confessio*, "who gave me such great grace that many people were reborn in God through me and afterward confirmed, and that clerics were ordained for them everywhere, for a people just coming to the faith." Later, he adds that he baptized "many thousands of people" and "ordained clerics everywhere," and that he cannot count the number of the sons and daughters of Irish kings who had become "monks and virgins of Christ."

The Irish of the fifth century had developed a sophisticated system of traditional law. They used an alphabet designed for carving on stone or wood rather than for writing in the modern sense. They were expert in working gold ornaments and bronze and iron weapons and utensils. The literary imagination that was to produce the first great sagas in any vernacular language in Europe and provide the basic themes for the literature of England and other neighboring lands was already being honed in the druidic schools. But the fact remains that the Irish were then a primitive people, largely nomadic, living on a combination of rudimentary agriculture, cattle raising, fishing, and gathering of berries, wild honey, and similar spontaneous bounties of nature. They had never built cities or towns, and their homes were mostly wooden or clay-walled huts. Patrick's descriptions of them as "savages," "heathens" worshiping "idols and things impure," and "barbarians" may have been influenced by his Roman concepts of civilization, but it cannot have been far wide of the mark.

Notwithstanding this evaluation of them as culturally inferior, Patrick did not hesitate either to identify with them or to give his new converts complete control of their church structures without any attempt to fit them first into his own molds. Later, they would struggle—as he did—to learn Latin and put in writing both in that language (used by scholars all across Europe) and in their native Gaelic a wealth of knowledge previously stored in the memory and passed orally from generation to generation. But all that followed long after the building of the Irish Church by Patrick on its own indigenous foundations.

It was a church significantly different in many of its practices from the churches of Gaul, created in the Roman forms, that was his starting point. He welcomed the Irish into the Church with their baggage of myths, rites, superstitions, and heritage, content to allow them the time to think through the contradictions between their moral judgments and practices and the dictates of Christ's teaching, and to make their adjustments without shattering their self-image and identity.

There was thus no abrupt rupture with the traditions and practices of the past. Celibacy was held in high honor, following the teaching of Saint Paul, yet a married clergy and even married bishops were accepted. Monogamy was presented as the Christian ideal, yet the practice of polygamy died out only in the sixteenth century, thanks to the combined efforts of the Council of Trent and Queen Elizabeth of England. Influenced undoubtedly by the tests of endurance to which aspirants to the status of warrior or Druid submitted themselves, a rigorous regime of penance and self-sacrifice was developed. Yet a tolerance for the weakness of the human condition was not lost, at least not until the British Government founded a major seminary at Maynooth in the early-nineteenth century and staffed it with Jansenistically influenced French priests who had fled their homeland during the French Revolution.

To detail the differences between the Church as founded by Patrick and the Irish Church of today is outside my present purpose. I cite these instances simply to illustrate my thesis that the approach to mission of this saint who lived over fifteen hundred years ago has stood the test of time. The missionaries, called by the Second Vatican Council to incorporate Christianity into every culture of the world by familiarizing themselves with the culture in question so that they can purify and guard it and also develop it in accordance with present-day conditions, have in Saint Patrick a model to study and imitate as well as an example of the success of this specific approach. The notion of missionary poverty, shockingly new when proclaimed by Ivan Illich in New York in the 1950s, is at least as old as Patrick.

# Thomas Becket

## (1118–70)

## JOEL WELLS

*Of Norman ancestry, son of Gilbert, sheriff of London, and Matilda, Thomas was born in London, studied at Merton priory in Surrey, and completed his studies at the University of Paris. In 1142, he entered the household of Theobald, archbishop of Canterbury, and soon became a favorite of the archbishop, who sent him on several missions to Rome and in 1144 to Bologna to study law under Gratian. In 1154 he was ordained deacon and then became archdeacon of Canterbury on the archbishop's nomination. He found favor in the eyes of Henry of Anjou when he convinced Pope Eugenius III not to recognize the succession of Eustace, son of Stephen, to the throne of England, thus ensuring Henry's claim to the throne as Henry II. In 1155 Henry appointed him chancellor of England, and he soon became the most powerful man in England next to Henry, known for the pomp and splendor of his style of life. He accompanied Henry on his military expedition to Toulouse in 1159 at the head of his own troops. In 1161, Theobald died and Henry named Thomas archbishop of Canterbury despite Thomas' objections. Thomas was elected in 1162, resigned the chan-*

cellorship against Henry's wishes, and was ordained a priest the day before he was consecrated archbishop. He changed his life-style completely, lived an austere life, and soon clashed repeatedly with the king over clerical and Church rights. In 1164 he refused to accept the Constitutions of Clarendon, denying among other things the rights of clerics to be tried in ecclesiastical courts and to appeal directly to Rome, and was forced to flee to France. He appealed to Pope Alexander III, but the Pope, not wishing to offend Henry, would not support him. When Henry and Thomas both remained adamant, Thomas, at the Pope's suggestion, retired to the Cistercian monastery at Pontigny, and when Henry objected, went to St. Columba abbey, near Sens, as the guest of King Louis VII of France. Finally, in 1170, Henry and Thomas patched up a truce in Normandy and Thomas returned to England. Disagreement soon broke out between the two over Thomas' suspension of the archbishop of York and the bishops who had officiated at the coronation of Henry's son, a violation of precedent since only the archbishop of Canterbury traditionally officiated at such a ceremony. Henry reacted violently, and in a fit of rage said he wished he was rid of this troublesome prelate; four of his knights took him at his word, and on the night of December 29 murdered the archbishop in his cathedral. The act shocked all of Europe, and Thomas was immediately proclaimed a martyr and in 1173 was declared a saint by Pope Innocent III. The following year, Henry made public penance at Thomas' shrine in Canterbury, though most historians agree he never intended Thomas to be murdered.

> ". . . the holy blissful martyr for to seek."
> CHAUCER
> *Canterbury Tales*

There was nothing blissful about the death of Archbishop Thomas Becket, whose shrine at Canterbury Cathedral

Chaucer's famous band of pilgrims journeyed toward. According to eyewitness reports such as that of Becket's clerk, William FitzStephen, it was truly the cruel and cold-blooded "murder in the cathedral" that T. S. Eliot dramatized so memorably in his play. Deserted by all but a few of the scores of monks he headed, he stood bravely to face the broadsword that crushed into his skull and, still conscious but prostrate, did not flinch from a second blow to the head delivered with such ferocity that after biting through the bone it broke against the stone. And having killed him, his assailants scrabbled the tips of their weapons inside his brain, as if beyond demolishing the man they wanted to cut out and mutilate his thoughts, his obdurate will.

To me, these gory details of Becket's death are significant, for somewhere among them may lie the proof and test of a proud man's decision, made and formed slowly but put to an instant test by the fact of terrorism: to accept death itself for a higher purpose, a purpose that Becket identified with the honor of God.

And because, too, without the violent death Thomas Becket might not, in the normal course of things, have been proclaimed a saint at all.

To understand it, a little backtracking is helpful. The quarrel between Henry II and Thomas Becket—an archbishop of the king's own creation—is a complex thicket of civil and ecclesiastical intrigue set inside a power struggle. Its twistings and devious turnings make the Watergate incident seem a straightforward affair. The immediate cause of the conflict between Church and state was the question of legal jurisdiction in the courts. The Church claimed that its courts governed the lives of ecclesiastics completely, in every area, and governed the lives of the laity in a wide range of other activities, as well; "those things which pertained to rule of souls" was the sweeping and hard-to-define premise. It maintained that the king and his nobility couldn't touch property or tax matters that involved church properties or people. Which, of course, didn't go down at all well with the king and his Lords.

The argument may seem strange and even silly to us now, but it was a deadly serious business in the twelfth century, when the papacy was seeking both to clearly establish its temporal as well as divine rights and to extend them into an ever wider sphere—including the then fringe areas of France and England.

To this end, the Pope was fighting the traditional practice of lay investiture, whereby a king could name his own bishops. Too often, of course, such men were the king's henchmen or relatives, inevitably chosen to do his will and bypass the Church's claims wherever possible. To enforce it, the Pope used many tactics, and always in reserve he held the trump of excommunication, of cutting off the recalcitrant or rebellious ruler from the life of the Church. This was, in those days, the ultimate weapon. For even if the king himself didn't care a fig, his almost universally Catholic subjects did.

So the scene was set for a clash as soon as any monarch felt he had the strength to weather such a confrontation. And such a king emerged in the strong, ambitious person of Henry II. He quickly solidified his rule in England, tightened his grip on his holding in France, and made it clear that he wanted to revoke many of the special privileges and tax exemptions which had been granted to the Church at the time of the Norman Conquest of England. To do this he needed to get more control over churchmen and church revenues, and he needed to be able to get at them legally, through his own courts.

What better way to begin than to install his own Lord Chancellor, trusted friend and adviser to the suddenly empty episcopacy of Canterbury, traditionally the head of the Church in England. This he did by naming Becket to become bishop in 1162 in the face of angry protest from the other bishops, who knew only too well what he was up to.

Thomas was baldly ordained a priest on one day and consecrated archbishop on the next. Henry had every reason to believe that he was on the high road to seeing his ambitions realized.

But the king had, to put it mildly, badly misjudged his man, for Thomas immediately resigned his chancellorship, took on an openly austere style of life, and made it clear that he took his new job very seriously indeed—from the Church's side—and would block any attempt to demolish the powers of the ecclesiastical courts.

Henry was hurt, baffled, and outraged. What had happened to his trusted Thomas? Thomas, whom he had helped make into the second-most-powerful as well as the second-wealthiest man in England? What miracle of grace had transformed him into this solemn-faced bishop? Or had Thomas simply been waiting for the chance, handed to him by the king on a golden platter, to push his own ambitions to the fore, once safely locked behind the wall of ecclesiastical immunity?

In the introduction to his excellent *The Life and Death of Thomas Becket* professor George Greenway, an expert on the period, says that despite the real trust and affection that had existed between the two men, Henry had never really understood the real Becket:

> There were depths in him which no man had plumbed. . . . Beneath his courtly exterior a genuine vein of religious piety ran deep within him. He had always, even in Henry's corrupt and venal court, kept his body chaste and his hands clean, and he practiced in secret the discipline of an ascetic. There is no need in his case to postulate a conversion in the usual sense of the word, a radical change in his moral character or in his mode of life: There is unbroken continuity of personality between Thomas the Chancellor and Thomas the Archbishop.*

* This and other direct quotations are taken from *The Life and Death of Thomas Becket*, translated and edited by George Greenway. © 1961 The Folio Society, Ltd., London.

Thomas was fourteen years older than the King, and Henry had somehow failed to grasp the iron that underlay his friend's dedicated and affable manner of serving him. He felt thoroughly betrayed and took up the challenge with a vengeance and fury, seizing properties and levying taxes and attacking the powers of the Church courts. Thomas responded by appealing to Rome and ran headlong into the political whirlwinds that were raging around the Pope's other struggles with other kings on the continent. Thomas went into exile. The long duel was engaged and the stage set for the eventual death of Becket.

It all came to a head in 1170, when a group of English bishops visited Henry at his court in France. He asked them how they thought he should best proceed with the intransigent archbishop of Canterbury. At first they told him not to put such questions to them, but to his own nobility and advisers. But one of them did comment that while Becket lived he doubted that the king would ever have his way—or experience a moment's peace, for that matter.

Edward Grim, a witness to the meeting, tells us that on hearing this, Henry was seized with such a fit of fury that he positively shook with rage.

"I have nourished and promoted in my realm idle and wretched knaves," screamed the king, "faithless to their lord, whom they suffer to be mocked thus shamefully by a low-born clerk."

This outburst was heard by many at the court, but four knights took it to heart, or at least saw it as a grand opportunity to curry favor with Henry. They decided to make of his tantrum a warrant to return to England and kill Thomas Becket.

They came to Canterbury with their armed followers on the twenty-ninth of December, broke into the archbishop's private quarters and threatened him, working up their nerve and rage in front of the terrified band of monks. They behaved erratically, like a teen-age gang, not quite sure how far they were willing to go in this holy compound, for they were committing sacrilege simply by being armed and there. Becket alone remained calm: "It will be easy to guard me; I will not run away," he told them.

The events that followed have been dramatized and recounted down through the centuries, and I will not recount them again. The point of special interest to me is that Thomas accepted death willingly, even knowing that these louts were perhaps acting more on their own than in the king's name. He couldn't be sure, of course. But he could have escaped and did not.

He could have saved himself even at the last moment, when the knights returned to attack him as he went to vespers in the cathedral. The testimony of his clerk, Fitz-Stephen, stresses the point: "Indeed, had he so wished, the archbishop might easily have turned aside and saved himself by flight, for both time and place offered an opportunity of escape without being found. It was evening, the long winter night was approaching, and the crypt was near at hand, where there were many dark and winding passages—or gone up to the roof of the cathedral by another door close at hand."

But Thomas stood his ground, nor did he resist, and he might have, for he had been a soldier and knew how to use a sword—though it would have been against his nature to partake in the desecration going on in the cathedral. Fitz-Stephen says he bore himself bravely, as a man without a care for what was about to happen to him—as if he was happy to have found a cause sufficiently honorable to die for.

So Thomas evidently had considered the ambiguity of his situation and discarded it as being finally irrelevant to his position. To run away from or to grovel and plead before the assassins, to stall and seek word or at least some sort of confirming information from the king—all would have been, in his eyes, to yield to terrorism. The knights would have doubtless killed him in any case; this way he died with his principles and dignity intact. Anything else would have been an insult to God's dignity.

For Thomas had convinced himself that in his steadfast opposition to the king's attacks on the powers of the Church he was indeed defending God's honor. It was a phrase that he used repeatedly in his negotiations and several attempts at compromise and reconciliation with the crown. And it had infuriated Henry at every instance. Thomas insisted on tacking on that final phrase, like a person determined to get the last word—I agree to everything we have discussed and will honor it as far as I can, "saving God's honor." By which he meant, and the king understood him to mean, except when what was involved seemed to Thomas to some way besmirch the honor of God.

There is danger and arrogance in that, of course, in identifying God's will directly with one's own. History is strewn with the carnage of despots who tried to sell themselves on that equation. But Thomas put no one but himself into the formula—he stood alone, and himself paid the ultimate price for his claim.

So Thomas comes down to us as a man more to be admired and respected than to be loved, perhaps; a saint by reason of martyrdom rather than as a holy man, guru, or mystic to inspire us to piety and abandonment to God's will.

But he may be more attuned to our time than those beloved "fools for God" who threw off the things of the world and followed a call. Not because he died for a cause that rouses much sympathy today—though, perversely, his death brought him immediate and clear-cut victory over Henry. (The enormous public outcry against the killing forced the king to restore all Church rights, to search out and execute the knights who killed Becket, to do public penance at Becket's tomb in the form of being scourged by the monks, and finally to let the ecclesiastical courts go their own way— so that when friend Chaucer was robbed repeatedly by the same band of brigands more than a century later, while he was about another king's business, one of the brigands was able to escape civil trial by "pleading his clergy," proving that he could read and write Latin and thus belonged to the Church's jurisdiction.)

Thomas died, as did his later counterpart Thomas More, for a principle that he would not yield or even bend in the face of force. That alone, in our time, when terrorism, hijacking, and kidnaping are increasingly the courts of last resort, should make him count for something in our eyes. He stood up to terrorism and found the strength of will to face it down even in ambiguous circumstances.

I also admire Thomas for refusing to become the king's pawn. It was Henry's own ambition and presumption and lack of insight that betrayed him, not Becket. Still, the pressure on Thomas to conform, to please the king, to go along with what he knew was expected, must have been enormous. To our age of conformity, peopled by those of us who so often succumb to such corporate and financial pressures in order to be "easy" and comfortable, his example speaks sharply.

Finally, I find Becket a saint far easier to identify with than most because he was not only a man of the world but full of common faults such as ambition, pride, and sometimes even stubborn arrogance. While by all accounts he lived a chaste life, he was, for a good many years, a devoted follower of the "good life." He built up his virtues slowly, overcoming his weaknesses as he matured—he received no great vision, nor was he knocked from his horse like Saul or granted mystic converse with God like Francis.

He made mistakes, got himself immersed in business, politics, and, even as a churchman, with political and ecclesiastical intrigue. He worked hard, met frustration often; in short, his life seems not too different from those which many of us lead. If Thomas Becket could achieve sanctity or at least salvation under such harried, ambiguous conditions simply by a gradual working and devotion to God's will as he saw it, then there may well be hope for us all.

# Dominic

## (1170–1221)

### TERE RIOS VERSACE

*Son of noble parents Felix Guzmán, royal warden of
Calaruega, and Joan of Aza, Dominic was born in Calaruega,
Spain, studied at the university at Palencia in 1184–95, was
probably ordained his last year there while pursuing his studies, and in 1199 assumed his canonry at Osma. In 1201 he
became prior superior of the chapter there, which was noted
for its strict discipline in following the Benedictine rule. In
1203, with Bishop Diego of Osma, he went to Languedoc,
where he preached widely against the Albigensians and helped
in the reform of the Cistercians there. In 1206 he founded
an institute for women at Prouille, in Albigensian territory,
and attached several preaching friars to it. When papal legate
Peter of Castelnau was murdered by the Albigensians, in
1208, Pope Innocent III launched a crusade against the Albigensians led by Count Simon IV of Montfort, which was
to go on for the next seven years. Dominic followed the
army, preaching to the heretics but with no great success. In
1214 De Montfort gave him a castle at Casseneuil, and
Dominic put into effect his plan for an order devoted to the
conversion of the Albigensians, with a group of six devoted*

*followers. Their foundation was approved by the bishop of Toulouse the following year, but Dominic was unsuccessful in getting his group established as an order of preachers at the Ecumenical Council in Rome in 1215. On his return to Toulouse his group adopted the Rule of St. Augustine and received papal approbation from Pope Honorius III in 1216, and the Order of Preachers (the Dominicans) was founded. Dominic spent the last years of his life organizing and expanding the order, traveling all over Italy, Spain, and France preaching, attracting new members, and establishing new houses. The order was tremendously successful in convert work, basing its approach on Dominic's concept of harmonizing the intellectual life with popular needs. He convoked the first general council of the order in Bologna in 1220 and died there the following year on August 6, after illness forced him to return from preaching to the pagans in Hungary. He was canonized in 1234. His feast day is celebrated on August 8.*

As a child, I thought he was three people: Dominic, Dominique, and Domingo. For a while I wondered about our friend Dominic Cansini, but he was classified properly as soon as I realized that he had a mustache and therefore couldn't be a saint. Saints in those days had beards or no beards, but never a dapper mustache.

Saint Dominic stood in a corner of the classroom at Dominican Academy in New York. His blond curls were always in place; his pale skin was tinged with rose at cheeks and chin; his blue eyes were rolled up as though he couldn't stand my behavior another minute.

Dominique was very French, faintly impish, and liked to gambol in *le parc du bon Dieu*. He lived only in my mind and took no particular form except that he was large and ungainly like me and would rather be playing knight-errant in the bamboo thicket than sitting in a classroom with his hands folded, knees together, and skirt pulled modestly over the knees.

If you think a bamboo thicket and a New York classroom are a strange combination, that's because you didn't grow up commuting between two islands: Manhattan and Puerto Rico.

So it was natural that the third person I thought he was, Domingo, was a high-nosed Spaniard very much like my father, who was loving but brooked no nonsense. Domingo charged about his world of Spain and southern France and northern Italy wreaking good and education on the helpless and ignorant.

Saint Dominic, who was always addressed by his proper title, came into my life—on a daily basis—in the fourth/sixth grade.

Dominican Academy, a very small school housed in brownstone, was struck one day in 1926 by an avalanche of Rios children. Seven Rios kids in a school of fewer than seventy-five children is a frighteningly high percentage.

All Rios children look alike to nuns in New York. They had great trouble telling us apart. On the first day of school, which is in any case compound confusion, we were told to line up outside the classroom we were assigned to. Towering over the other kids in the fourth-grade line, I watched my older sister Kayo, tiny and fragile, disappear among the bigger kids in the sixth-grade line.

A flurried nun came dashing along the hall straightening everyone out. Spotting the monster in the fourth-grade line, and the tiny Rios in the sixth-grade line, she snatched us out and switched us, putting me in sixth and Kayo in fourth.

Our brothers thought it was funny. Kayo didn't mind, because she was an Artist. Even at that tender age her paintings were impressive. Family friends were asking for them and hanging them in places of honor. Being in the fourth grade meant that Kayo wouldn't have to do so much homework and could spend more time painting. I was ecstatic. My wild imagination cut two years off the confinement of schooling and gave it to daydreaming.

We all kept quiet about the switch. Kayo didn't like answering to Teresa, particularly the way they pronounced it, like a squeaking mouse: Chreesa. She put up with it, though, for the sake of her Art.

I managed to stay in the sixth grade for three months by shooting my hand up every time I knew the answer to a question. The sister would say agreeably, "Now, Catherine" (it was a much prettier name than Chressa), "we must give the other children a chance."

Kayo and I got great marks right up to examination time, when it became painfully evident that "Catherine" in no way belonged in the sixth grade.

We were subjected to cross-examination by fourth-grade, sixth-grade, and principal-type nuns; father and mother; and a bit of harassment from the cook, who thought we were all too big for our britches.

Back I went to the fourth grade, where I towered over the other kids but had to sit up front, where the nun could keep an eye on me.

At school there were discussions, long, one-sided, and detailed, of honesty, embezzlement, decency, selfishness, boldness, haughtiness, and sin.

Our mother said, over and over, "Oh, darlings, how could you?"

Our father said coldly we'd better none of us try anything like that again.

The cook said she always knew we were all too big for our britches anyway.

Sitting at the feet of Saint Dominic, I got to know him pretty well. He stood there in his black-and-white robes and raised his eyes at my perfidy for a whole year.

He would never have behaved the way I had. He was holy and never had a mean thought and wouldn't dream of hitting his brother over the head with a ukulele or smearing black shoe polish on his foot to hide a hole in his stocking.

One night, on the ship going to Puerto Rico, I dreamed he was standing in the corner of the cabin and when the ship rolled, he fell over with a crash and his rolled-up eyes stared out at me from the mess of broken plaster. I woke up screaming and trying to get out of the cabin without opening the door.

That was when Domingo showed up. It was explained that even if he were standing in a corner of the cabin, he would never hurt a child. He was a Spanish gentleman, and it was the obligation of such to protect children. "Domingo was a brilliant man. He wanted people to learn. You can ask him to help you with your homework. He taught priests and nuns and even Pope Innocent. Anyone who would listen."

In San Juan we went to a dim church and looked at the statue there. Sure enough, since this statue had been made in Spain, he had rugged, sharp features and olive skin, dark eyes, and black hair. He looked like someone I might even know.

Lo and behold, the day I went to school in San Juan, Sister Dominica was teaching the music class! It was she who introduced me to Domingo's friend Tomás de Aquino, one of the greatest brains in history. I should talk to him, she said, when I had troubles with music, which baffled me because I'm tone-deaf. It didn't seem as if anyone like him would want anything to do with someone whose own kin flinch when she "sings."

Sister said she didn't think that would bother Tomás and that maybe he even might help me to tell the difference between *Pange Lingua* and *Adeste Fideles* without looking at the music sheets.

She sang at the top of her lungs, but when she talked she whispered, and in rapid-fire Spanglish she told me that Saint Dominic was wonderful and that anyone who belonged to him was wonderful too. She told me about Rose of Lima and Vicente Ferrer and a dozen more. And topped it off with, "And I am going to give *you* to him and he will watch over you all your life."

Then she brought out whom she considered the best of Domingo's boys: Martin de Porres. Spanish-polite, she whispered, "I hadn't suggested him to you before," as though she were presenting a not quite suitable suitor, "because you are really quite intelligent, you only have a very short attention span. Many of Martin's superiors thought *he* was quite stupid. But he loved God, so that he was given the special gift of bilocation: the ability to be in two places at once."

Now, *there* was a fellow that fired my imagination. Dominic and Tomás were smart and besides could pay attention for more than a few seconds at a time. But just in case Domingo wanted to help me out now and then so I could get through an exam without daydreaming, I began to talk to Martin. In case he really was dumb, he could ask Domingo.

Just as I would say to one of my brothers, whose mental processes our father respected, "Hey, ask Dad if—" I now said to Martin, "Hey, ask Domingo if he won't help me concentrate today." No use asking Martin for that: he had a reputation of being as stupid as I, only he was holy.

It was the beginning of a long friendship. Martin stood by me when I had to give up the German shepherd Fritz, who was so beautiful when he ran that it hurt to look at him. And Martin must have talked to Dominic about the bone pain, because together they helped me think of something else while it was going on.

Then I married a dashing lieutenant and together we produced five splendid, intelligent, handsome, graceful people with long attention spans who could carry a tune. God must have pretended not to notice my genes.

Early on, the splendid five got on with my friends. They rather tended to prefer Domingo, and I went along with that but kept Martin on the side. I told about them, and the kids retold the stories to their friends. Domingo had done this and Tomás had done that, and Martin could talk to animals and be in two places at once.

One day in Germany, where drivers all seem to be demolition-derby winners, our car stalled. In the middle of a six-lane high-speed avenue, with the rear seat filled with kids, that demented vehicle took a notion into its head to drop dead. Horns tooted, people shouted, and the traffic snarled. Enraged drivers tried to lane-jump around us. Brakes squealed. The ignition didn't even make contact. The children were scared, I hit the panic button.

In a flustered rage I yelled, "Okay, Saint Martin, see what you can do about *this!*"

I swear it, it happened. A young man in a leather jacket ran the four lanes of automotive obstacle course from the sidewalk, opened the car door on my side, shoved me over, stepped on the starter, and the motor roared into action. He jumped out, snapped a heel-clacking bow at us, and dodged back through the snarled traffic to safety on the sidewalk.

We got off that steeplechase and onto a side street, where things were quieter.

A small voice from the back seat quavered, "Mom, was that *really* Saint Martin?"

I really couldn't say, but I know what I think.

Dominic and his friends kept in touch with us even when we forgot them. Through the years he was like a family friend. We told the stories to the kids, and they began to talk about him as though they knew him. When my first book was published I got a little drunk with power and decided to write a life of Saint Dominic for grown-up children. In Madison, Wisconsin, there wasn't much material available. A pilgrimage to the Dominican friary there produced a long epic poem about him—in Old French. Home, curled up with an Old French book, it was electrifying to discover that Old French, instead of being another language, just hadn't been divorced from Spanish yet. I could read it!

Then came the agony. Writing a biography wasn't the happy daydreaming process that writing fiction was. You had to check the facts and stick to them. And keep those chapters sorted and straight. Chapters were outlined on wrapping paper taped to the basement wall—about fourteen feet of it. The actual chapters were laid out on the living-room floor for sorting and realignment. The whole family went stark raving crackers, but finally it was finished and off to the publisher, who passed it to some Dominican sisters for appraisal.

Dominic's friends the sisters thought it was terrible. They said, in effect, I should stick to telling little stories and forget such grandiose ideas as writing biographies.

I'm no person to be receiving messages from on high, but if that wasn't a message I've never seen one. Properly abashed, I went back to writing about nuns that fly and people who live in mausoleums.

The family relaxed; we lived in a dozen or so states and a few foreign countries. Rocky, our eldest son, graduated from West Point and was transferred to Korea. Steve went into the Army too, Dick went to the Coast Guard, Mike and Tracy were both in school. Hum, the dashing lieutenant, had developed into a distinguished colonel and was transferred to Fort Sheridan, Illinois, where we lived in an old stone house overlooking Lake Michigan.

A new chaplain arrived on post. Mike, now eleven years old, came home from serving daily Mass chuckling.

"Guess what," he said. "I thought Father Joe didn't know how to say Mass, and I tried to tell him how, and you know what? He's a Dominican, and they *all* say Mass backwards."

It finally got straightened out that Dominicans had been granted a special dispensation to say Mass a little more quickly so they'd have more time for study. Mike was all for that, and decided then and there to become a Dominican. (He didn't.)

As people do when they get older, I got sick and was confined to bed for a long time. Dominic's boy Father Joe brought me an interesting book to read: the *Summa!*

Too weak to lift the tome (it was only the first volume of ten), I kept falling asleep with it on my stomach. When Father came back a week later and saw I was still on page three, he took the tome away and brought me the *Companion to the Summa.*

Books have been my friends and my companions, but because of that short attention span, early on in life I became an accomplished description skipper. I could bomb through *David Copperfield* in a day and a half by flipping through the pages to the action and dialogue. That's what Dominic's boy found me doing with the *Companion*: skipping the heavy stuff. He took that away and brought *My Way of Life*, Walter Farrell's condensation of his condensation of the *Summa*.

*My Way of Life* became a part of our household and so much a part of my life that it was reading book, prayer book, and guidebook. When my husband had a series of strokes and heart attacks, he wanted that book read to him when he could listen to nothing else.

But Dominic didn't just send me a guidebook and let me go; he stayed on duty. When Rocky decided to give up the Army and go for the priesthood, it was a Dominican who pointed the way.

And when Rocky was captured by the Viet Cong and was being tortured and it became clear that he would never be released, and the father of the family became so ill that his son had to take over, when it seemed as if there would never be anything to smile at again, a Maryknoller sent me a record.

"Would you do me a favor and translate this for me?" he wrote.

Grateful for anything that would occupy my mind and still let me stay home to watch over my sick ones and wait for some kind of message from the Department of Defense, I began to play the record.

The Belgian French was hard to understand, so I had to play it over and over. The gay little tune filled the house and lifted everyone's spirits.

"Dominique, Dominique. . . ."

Don't forget us, Dominique, Dominic, Domingo.

# Francis of Assisi

## (c. 1181–1226)

### JOHN S. KENNEDY

*Probably no other saint has affected so many in so many different ways as Francis of Assisi, by his devotion to poverty, his concern for the poor, and his delight in God's works as revealed in nature. The son of a wealthy merchant, Peter Bernardone, he was born either late in 1181 or early 1182 in Assisi, Italy. He was christened John by his mother, Pica, while his father was on a business trip, but his father renamed him Francis on his return. Francis spent his youth as an exuberant pleasure seeker, went gaily to war, was taken prisoner in 1202, and on his release went back to his carefree ways. After suffering a serious illness he returned to the wars, in 1205, but a vision he experienced in Spoleto changed his life. He made a pilgrimage to Rome in 1206 and then devoted himself to a life of poverty and the care of the sick and the poor. He was denounced by his father, who disinherited him for the life he had embraced. After repairing several churches, he retired to a little chapel, the Portiuncula, attracted several leading citizens to his way of life, and in 1210 secured verbal approval, for a rule he had drawn up, from Pope Innocent III. He quickly attracted numerous followers and in 1212 was* joined by Clare despite the violent objections of her family. He was shipwrecked on his way to Syria to preach to the Mohammedans and was unsuccessful in a second attempt when he fell ill in Spain while on the way to Morocco. He obtained the famous Portiuncula indulgence from Pope Honorius III in 1216, convened the first general chapter of his order in 1217 to organize the huge numbers of his followers, and in 1219 sent his first missionaries to Tunis and Morocco. He himself went to Egypt but was unsuccessful in an attempt to convert Sultan al-Malik al-Kamil and then was obliged to hasten back to Italy to combat a movement in the order to mitigate his original rule of simplicity, humanity, and poverty. He resigned as head of the order in 1220 but revised the rule of the order and secured its approval by Pope Honorius III in 1223. That same year, he built a crib at Christmas, establishing a custom still widely followed at Christmas. In 1224, while praying in his cell at Mt. Alverno, he received the stigmata, the climax of a series of visions and supernatural events he had experienced throughout his life. He died in Assisi on October 3 and was canonized in 1228. Interestingly enough, Francis was never ordained. Francis composed many prayers, some of which, such as "Canticle of Brother Sun" and his prayer for peace have become spiritual classics together with The Little Flowers of St. Francis, a collection of stories about Francis and his followers, by Brother Ugolino di Monte Santa Maria, one of his followers. His feast day is celebrated on October 4.

It took me almost thirty years to get to Assisi. In aspiration, I had started toward the Umbrian hill town when I was in high school. One of my teachers, Father John H. Anderson, had made his seminary course in Rome and was enamored of Italy. He often spoke of Italy, describing its beauty so graphically as to cast a spell on his listeners, certainly on me.

Of Assisi he conjured up an image that was imprinted on

my mind and heart. Everything he said about Assisi centered in and radiated from Francis.

Because of his talks, Italy haunted my imagination. I longed to go there and experience its wonders firsthand. Would I ever be able to do so? I feared not. I would probably die before I could make that most desirable of journeys.

Dr. Anderson must have perceived the effect his words had on me. At any rate, he asked me to write an article on Francis for the school magazine. He gave me a copy of G. K. Chesterton's book *St. Francis of Assisi.*

This was my introduction to Chesterton. He enchanted me, and he furthered my enchantment with Francis. I ground out the article, its facts cribbed from Chesterton, its tone and form my own juvenile fault. I suppose that I might look it up in the school library, but have decided against that, to avoid embarrassment. The sins of one's adult life are hard enough to bear.

But adult life does bring perspective, and even sometimes a portion of wisdom, impossible in youth. My original conception of Francis was largely romantic. Had he not set out, brilliantly caparisoned, to win knighthood? That was splendid, but so, too, was his conversion to the service of God. It was so dramatic: the casting off of his finery, his defiance of his father, his assumption of garb fit only for a beggar, his wandering through springtime landscapes singing the divine praises and the marvels of an unspoiled world, his communication with birds and beasts, his gathering a company of kindred spirits, and above everything else, his living of the pristine gospel. Gallantry, gaiety, clean decisiveness, and limpid Christian simplicity.

The idyllic in all this would appeal to a young person, and so would the protest against, and the renunciation of, the carious, oppressive established order. Release, freedom—Francis represented these. He struck out in new directions, yet he did so by return to the old truths announced and exemplified by Christ.

I knew, of course, about the stigmata, the duplicating in

Francis' body of the wounds of Christ. But even this was seen sentimentally, and as a kind of rapturous culmination of a relatively short life, since he died when he was about forty-four. It was a heroic touch, a precious seal of approval, lightly applied and flattering to the recipient.

At the time, I knew no Franciscans, had not even seen one. But I had some acquaintance with another religious community of men that practiced poverty, led an ascetic life, and had a habit not unlike that to be seen in pictures of Francis. I thought of joining that community, and even disclosed this intention to some friends, pleased to be impressing them with my capacity for sacrifice. I also thought of becoming an actor, but dropped no word of that. Which proves, I think, that I had no serious appreciation of Francis.

I did not enter any religious community, but became a diocesan priest and, eventually, that mythical monster, a monsignor. I hope I did not become an actor.

Over the years, other books about Francis appeared, lengthier, more scholarly, more detailed than Chesterton's. As they came along, I read them. They extended my knowledge of the saint. He became ever more attractive, more endearing, as well as more relevant, in a practical way, to my own life and times.

His adult life was spent in the thirteenth century, which some have idealized as the greatest, meaning the most Christian, of centuries. There is a tendency to visualize it as set in a Renaissance painting aglow with color and peopled by quaint figures, as a kind of perpetual pageant animated by an incorrupt faith.

It did have its admirable qualities, and the Church was then a major power. But it was also an era brutal in many respects. War was waged almost without intermission up and down the Italian Peninsula, with no quarter given. Towns were sacked, harvest fields burned, civilians savaged, prisoners of war mutilated. The poor were legion, and they were trampled by the rich.

The Church may have been formidable and prosperous in

temporal terms. But it was in crying need of reform. Prelates were, many of them, secular rulers and warriors, and lived in grand style. Great numbers of the clergy were ill-educated and preached seldom and wretchedly; scandal was common.

These conditions inevitably affected the lives of the people, who, uninstructed and given bad example, had but a meager knowledge of Christian teaching and the feeblest incentive to the practice of virtue.

Francis stood out against this disorder. Having taken part in warfare and been himself a prisoner of war, he renounced the use of arms or of any kind of force. He preached peace and served as peacemaker between rival towns that had been brawling for generations.

He was convinced that he had a vocation to contribute to reform of the Church. But he did not rail at abuses, excoriate those in authority, engage in controversy, meddle with doctrine, or propose any elaborate scheme of structural renewal. He went about enunciating the gospel in homely language, and his words struck his hearers of all degrees to the quick—the mighty and the lowly alike.

More telling than his words was his example. He lived what he preached. It was this that lent his words their weight. He dressed by choice as the poorest of the poor did of necessity.

He and his associates were without possessions and begged their bread in the streets of whatever town they found themselves in. He and they had no permanent home, but sheltered in huts or caves. His solicitude for the stricken, as in his personal care of dreaded, isolated lepers, was regular and tender.

If his words registered because of his conduct, this in turn was energized by his prayer and penance. We are repeatedly told of his resort to prayer, the hours he spent alone with God, questioning and listening, praising and petitioning. He was always mortified. He deplored penitential excess and forbade it to his companions. But he was strict in self-discipline, because he had a horror of sin.

One wonders whether, were he to appear in our age of violence, of infidelity, of senseless indulgence and waste, of moral callousness, and of a Church in need of renewal, he would have the impact he did in his own time. Present conditions would probably require some accommodation in method. But his spirit, his fundamental approach, would not have dated.

Those who would change the Church to make it conform more closely to the gospel and to win a hearing from the world could learn from his Christian civility, his unsparing self-scrutiny, his persuasive embodiment of what he urged on others, his example of prayer and penance.

Above all, what is to be learned from him now is the primacy of the love of God. He is a capital exemplar of love of neighbor, and this precisely because he sought first to give God the love that is his due. It was from love of God that St. Francis saw all goodness flowing, and he was habitually concerned to search out the will of God and to do it.

In our age, the tendency is to reverse the order of the great commandments and even to drop the first one altogether. It is assumed that humanitarianism can be self-sustaining, which is like expecting a plant to go on flowering after it has been severed from its roots.

I began by saying that it took me almost thirty years to get to Assisi. I now perceive that it has taken me several hundred words to get there in this essay.

Get to Assisi I did, the first time almost a quarter of a century ago. My friend Monsignor Joseph R. Lacy was then stationed in Rome, and thanks to him, we drove up from there to the town of St. Francis.

The reality of a place long imagined can be disappointing, at least initially. I found this to be true of Rome, which I had envisioned as classical or medieval, not realizing that it was now a modern metropolis with some leavings of its ancient self. The Rome that was must be sifted from the Rome that is.

But Assisi is different. As one approaches it across a spacious and fertile plain, one espies it perched on a flank of Monte Subasio. From a distance it is seen as a picturesque unity, a consistent and charming whole, and it does not let one down upon arrival.

It was early evening when we arrived. We sat out on the broad terrace of a hotel at the edge of town. From there we could look across the green countryside and see farm workers returning from their fields, smoke rising from the chimneys of houses which at that remove seemed diminutive, scores of swallows wheeling and plummeting against the expanse of sunset sky. Church bells sounded, now in harmony, now in dissonant contention. From below could be heard people talking and laughing, a woman calling to a child, someone singing.

We took a first walk through the town after dinner, up and down meandering cobblestone streets that were steep, narrow, and dimly lighted. Lining them solidly were old stone houses, with façades that bore traditional local features such as the *porta dei morti*, the door used only when a dead person is carried out for burial.

We went into the main square, the scene of revels in which Francis avidly took part when he was a rich and worldly young man. Here, as elsewhere in Assisi, it seemed possible to catch glimpses of Francis at one or another stage of his life, so little has Assisi changed over the centuries and so charged is it with his presence.

Our walk brought us to one of the town gates. Beyond it, in the deep darkness, a few men were quietly conversing. The night was vast and tranquil. A feeling of peace prevailed.

So began the first of several visits to Assisi. Whenever I was in Italy thereafter I saw to it that I got to Assisi, if only for a few hours. The town and its environs speak of Francis as few other places do of their celebrated sons or daughters.

The hotel in which I stayed is close to the massive, three-tiered basilica named for him. This church-upon-a-church-upon-a-church abounds in things to see and to reflect on. Its wall paintings, a succession of masterpieces by Giotto and others, unfold the story of Francis' life. Magnificent though they are, I have found them less impressive than a habit worn by Francis and now displayed behind glass.

Many European cathedrals have their treasuries containing exquisite jeweled sacred vessels, bishops' rings and crosses, and sumptuous antique brocade vestments. These may dazzle the eye but leave one cold. But no one can look with indifference at this single coarse garment worn threadbare.

It conveys something of the actuality of the poverty to which Francis was wed. Nothing glamorous about it, nothing of playacting or an evening's masquerade. That stark habit concretizes the renunciation that Francis made for the sake of treasure that does not perish.

During one visit to Assisi, I went into the basilica on a Sunday morning hoping to offer Mass at one of the small altars in the crypt. Usually there were many priests waiting for a turn. But on this day, at this hour, I was the only priest in the whole place. Not merely that, the priest assigned to offer a scheduled Mass at the main altar just in front of the tomb of Francis had, unaccountably, not shown up. I was asked to substitute for him, which I did, with a sense of privilege and a feeling of joy.

The joy of Francis is proverbial, but one hears far less of his sufferings. Yet the two are vitally connected. He met repeated rebuffs and humiliations, was misunderstood and thwarted, went through periods of troubled conscience. He was afflicted with all manner of physical ailments, never enjoyed good health, and toward the end was blind and in excruciating pain.

But he maintained that spiritual joy is as necessary to the soul as blood to the body. He regarded his sufferings as a purification that was a necessary preliminary to genuine, unquenchable joy. He would not tolerate glumness in his first followers and was forever exhorting them to be joyful in the Lord.

His joy burst forth in song. His "Canticle of the Sun" has a secure place in world literature. In it he pours out his praise and thanks to God for the good things and the glories of earth and sky, which, though generally taken for granted or ignored, witness to the goodness and glory of God.

One might suppose that he composed this canticle in the exuberance of youth. Not so. It came only toward the close of his life. He fashioned it at the chapel of San Damiano, where, years before, he had first recognized his vocation and determined to pursue it.

The visitor to San Damiano today sees the place much as it was in Francis' day. There is an opening in a wall that looks out upon sunswept hillside and plain, a breath-taking view that might well inspire praise of the Maker of all.

Then one remembers that when Francis composed the joyous canticle, he could not see that view. His sight had dwindled away. He was weak and in unrelieved agony. Those with him thought that death was near for the poor, anguished remnant of skin and bone he had become. But his spirit could soar in lyrical delight.

He had but lately returned to Assisi from a month of prayer and fasting on the lonely summit of Monte della Verna. This period of solitude and contemplation had been climaxed by his reception of the stigmata. He had meditated on the Passion of Christ year in, year out, and now he had been branded with its marks.

His long journey toward Love was almost completed. He had at last toiled all the way up the hill of Calvary and was about to pass beyond it. His sufferings now exceeded any he had previously experienced. But he continued to sing until his heart faltered to a halt.

To appreciate Francis fully, one must follow him all the way, not stopping at this or that vignette: his preaching to the birds, his taming of the wolf of Gubbio, his introducing the Christmas crèche. His gallantry, his jests, his dancing please us and make us smile, but there is much more to him than these. He has sometimes been reduced to hardly more than an enthusiast for the great outdoors, or a troubadour in tatters, or a blessed, skipping simpleton, or a naïve relic of an age outgrown.

The fact is that he went to the heart of the matter in all that matters in any age, ours included. Someone has said that Francis made the gospel live in Umbria. It can be made to live anywhere, at any time, by Christians who, imitating him, will strive and suffer to assimilate it, personify it, and apply it in their own sphere.

# Joan of Arc—'Go Boldly'

## (1412–31)

## CANDIDA LUND

*The daughter of Jacques d'Arc, a peasant farmer, Joan was one of five children and was born on January 6 in Domrémy, France. A pious child, she was only thirteen when she experienced the first of her supernatural visions. As time went on, she identified the voices she heard as those of St. Michael, St. Catherine, St. Margaret, and others who, she claimed, revealed to her that her mission was to save France. The French commander at Vaucouleurs laughed at her attempt to convince him in 1428 that her visions were genuine. But when prophecies she made came true, she was sent the following year to the dauphin, son of the insane King Charles VI, who preferred a life of pleasure to mounting the throne with all its responsibilities after his father's death, in 1422. Her recognition of the dauphin, though he was disguised, and a secret signal she gave him, convinced him of the authenticity of her mission. She was allowed to lead an expedition to Toulouse and, clad in a suit of white armor, led her forces to victory. She persuaded the dauphin to be crowned King Charles VII in Rheims on July 17, with herself at his side. The coronation and then her expedition relieving the*

*siege of Orléans electrified and revivified all of France. In the
spring of 1430 she set out on a new campaign but was captured near Compiègne on May 24 and sold to the English by
the Duke of Burgundy on November 21. She was charged
with heresy and witchcraft before the court of Bishop Pierre
Cauchon, and her visions were declared to be diabolical. She
was tricked into a form of recantation on May 23, 1431, but
when she dressed again in male attire, which she had agreed
to abandon, she was condemned as a lapsed heretic and
burned at the stake at Rouen on May 30, the victim of her
enemies' determination to do away with her. A court appointed by Pope Callistus III found her innocent in 1456,
and she was canonized in 1920. Two years later, she was declared patroness of France.*

Rather early in life, I concluded that it was necessary to pick
heavenly friends with meticulous care. I needed to like them
very much in addition to respecting them, this last, at its
lowest level, coming under the dullish heading Christian
Duty. In choosing my sainted friends, I looked for compati-
bility. This narrowed, if such is mathematically possible, my
circle of celestial intimates. It nevertheless has been a circle
that has stood the test of time.

An important person in this secret circle is Joan of Arc. In
the beginning she was a new and exciting person whom I was
meeting for the first time. By now she is an old and treasured
friend whose reactions to happenings today I can predict and
into whose mouth I can put words on such subjects as
women's rights, the armaments race, ordination of women,
and the duties of the hierarchy.

I am not certain that I do not sometimes mix up the historical Joan with the legendary Joan. No matter. Thucydides
said that in his *History of the Peloponnesian War* he related
the speeches made by the principal participants, but where
he had no record, he provided the speeches they should have
given in the circumstances. He held that this, too, was history.

I empathize with his position. Where I am most likely to transfer the literary Joan into a living being is from George Bernard Shaw's *St. Joan*. Shaw's Joan breathes for me, and anything he has her say or do has become, for me, history. She is as real as the Joan of the trial record; I call upon Thucydides for support of my position.

Few women in history have had more written about them than Joan of Arc. She has been identified as the central figure of a whole literature of controversy. I am chary about the person who stimulates no controversy or who produces no animus. Such a person sounds a little too much like blancmange. I once heard of a novice mistress whom everyone liked, and I have always wondered about her. Among the contributors to the literature of controversy on Joan have been Shakespeare (unless Henry VI is pseudo-Shakespearean), Voltaire, Quicherat, Lang, Mark Twain, Anatole France, Paine, Bernanos, Péguy, Anouilh, Vita Sackville-West, and, of course, Shaw. And books keep pouring forth. There is an American cardinal who had, at one time, over three thousand books on Joan of Arc in his library.

Biography is said to be a continuing process. New material, new approaches, can justify a new biography. With Joan, however, I think it has been more than that. It is as though each age wishes to claim her for its own. Since her death, over five hundred years ago, there has been hardly a generation to which she has not served as a fresh example.

In my time it was not surprising to see General de Gaulle, as the herald of the French Resistance, invoke the memory of Joan of Arc. His supporters claimed he turned to her for inspiration because both had a mystic view of France's destiny and sacred rights. His opponents felt he was not above exploiting her. His detractors said mockingly, "The man believes he is Joan of Arc."

Across the Channel, Winston Churchill called Joan an angel of deliverance, the noblest patriot of France, and declared all soldiers should read her story and ponder it. One should not lose sight of the fact that he was speaking of the ancient foe. Nor should one forget that Joan and Sir Winston held in common their difficulty in getting along with generals. Both felt that they knew better than their generals how battles should be conducted, but they were unable to persuade the generals to see it their way. Churchill's admiration of Joan has been emulated by the English people, and not only by the English. In 1976, the two million visitors to Madame Tussaud's Wax Museum, in London, were asked to name the person they most admired. Joan of Arc received the highest number of ballots, and Winston Churchill was second.

Every person has particular reasons for being drawn to another. What is it that has drawn me to Joan? First of all, I like her. The saints who stir me must be my friends, not icons. Joan is not an icon (although she makes a splendid subject for artists, witness Rouault's heroic figure, and paintings were made of her even during her lifetime). Why do I like her? I like her because she is more woman than lady. I prefer my saints to be women and my sinners to be ladies. I like her for her virtues, which are admirably warm and human virtues writ large. In her I find purposefulness, piety, salty wit, naturalness, shrewdness, courage, clear thinking, confidence in God, leadership, strong-mindedness, a high sense of duty, and a love of freedom. Not the usual litany of virtues found in saints. Indeed qualities sometimes found in villains. How, then, can these be considered the virtues of a saint? The answer to that is the manner in which Joan used them. She simply put in tandem God and practical affairs, whether political or military.

Important also for me is that Joan was a woman possessed of these virtues. Centuries before women joined together to seek full recognition of their rights, Joan moved, assured and determined because she was confident in God, in a man's world. It has been heartening to know that this was done in the fifteenth century, even though it required divine inspiration. Her man's world for two short years—from her seventeenth year to her nineteenth—included the royal court, army camps, battlefields, prison, and the trial court. Those years found her at Vaucouleurs, Chinon, Orléans, Rheims, the outskirts of Paris, Compiègne, Rouen. I think of her, during those years and in those places, as being measured by her king, by her army, by her judges, and finally, in a sense, by her executioner. She was far removed from a usual frame of reference, yet her behavior makes it easy to identify with her, not because I think I would behave like her, but because I wish I could.

Joan felt called by God to save France. Her voices gave her this message, and she in turn gave it to all who needed to know. Her singleness of purpose as she responded to this call was evident constantly. To achieve her end she first had to persuade the dauphin to be crowned King of France. From Robert de Baudricourt in his castle at Vaucouleurs, she sought help to reach the dauphin at Chinon. It was the steward of Baudricourt, "scanty of hair, scanty of flesh," who sensed the mettle of Joan before his blustery master. Said the steward to the squire, "She is so positive, sir." There is something about this statement that gives a modern ring. There is something about it, too, that helps me to square my shoulders when necessary and jut my jaw.

The dauphin was as lacking in purpose and positive thinking as Joan was endowed. He was, however, a practical joker. Thus, he is supposed to have heightened the drama of Joan's visit to his court by placing another on his throne and betaking himself to the anonymous ranks of his courtiers. He must have thought his court would awe a country lass. He did not know his country lass. Even without feeling she was divinely guided, Joan's enviable naturalness would have left her feeling at home in court. Someone wrote of Queen Elizabeth II that she constrains her emotions for the sake of her dignity. Joan's dignity lay in her naturalness, that is, in being herself and giving full play to her emotions.

Later, before her judges, she was to say that when she had to see the king, she was told by her voices, "Go boldly: when thou art before the king he shall have a good sign to receive

and believe in thee." Go boldly she did, and provided a
motto of courage for women to adopt whatever role.

To pick out Charles would have been no great feat; she
would have needed only to look for the sorriest figure there,
sans eyebrows and nearly sans eyelashes. Imbuing him with
confidence and direction was, however, a much worthier
achievement. She told him she brought news from God. She
assured him that God would restore his kingdom, would have
him crowned at Rheims, and would expel his enemies. She
was God's messenger to that effect. She urged him to set her
boldly to work (again that magnificent motto), and she
would raise the siege of Orléans. Within nine months she
had accomplished this and had stood by the dauphin as he
was crowned King of France.

In his play, Shaw used the scene in the ambulatory of the
cathedral of Rheims after the coronation as the setting in
which Joan's voices spoke again to her in the quarter-hour
chiming of the cathedral bells. At the quarter, "Dear-child-of-
God." At the half-hour, "Be-brave-go-on." At the three-
quarters, "I-am-thy-Help." And at the hour, "God will save
France." I can remember a particularly trying winter when I
frequently said those lines to myself, although it was not
France that I felt needed saving. I even went so far as to tack
the lines up in a corner of my closet so they could emit to me
waves of courage and confidence in God.

Just as Joan put fight into the dauphin and has put fight
into me, so did she put fight into the French soldiers. One of
the charges, the 53rd Article, to be brought against her later,
claimed:

> The said Jeanne, against the bidding of God and His
> Saints, proudly and presumptuously assumed domina-
> tion over men; she appointed herself leader and captain
> of an army which rose at times to the number of 16,000
> men, in which there were princes, barons, and other no-
> bles, all of whom she made fight under herself as princi-
> pal captain.

This charge is not without an amusing aspect: sixteen thousand men, including the proud nobles of the land, following the maid against their will! How could these men have been compelled to follow her? Such a charge is not flattering to the soldiers whom she led.

With the soldiers Joan was at ease. She talked their language, but devoid of oaths. She described a distance as being a "lance length." She dressed as they did, and at some cost to her reputation. George Bernard Shaw called her "the pioneer of rational dressing for women," but there were contemporaries of Joan who did not feel this way. No twentieth-century nun—and I speak from at least small experience—exchanging her habit for mufti in order to work more effectively has had to answer more questions than Joan dressed in man's attire. When asked if God ordered her to wear a man's dress, she answered that dress is the least thing, but that she wore male attire and carried arms at God's bidding.

The soldiers who were her companions-at-arms did not expect her to dress other than she did. They saw her when necessary sleep in open fields and always in full armor. When possible, with a woman as her companion, she slept in a tent or a hut, not because she sought greater comfort (little enough comfort either way), but because it was more seemly.

Although Joan bore arms, she declared that she had never killed a man. She pointed out that her standard meant more to her than her sword. She bore the standard when attacking the enemy so as not to be tempted to kill anyone.

Her outdoor life deepened her love of being free. When a prisoner, she candidly admitted that "It is true that I wished and still wish to escape, as is lawful for any captive or prisoner." She preferred dying to being chained.

She was captured at Compiègne by the Burgundians. For a handsome sum, they sold her to the Duke of Warwick. This, however, was not before she had attempted to escape from the tower by hanging from the window by her stretched arms and letting herself drop sixty feet. She dropped, of course, into unconsciousness and recapture. By attempting to escape, she went contrary to her voices, but I have always found something appealing in the brash girl who, gravely disturbed over the slaughter in Compiègne and terrified about falling into English hands, was willing to take a chance. One is not always right. Nor does one always acquiesce.

It was at her trial that Joan's wit, shrewdness, and clear thinking were brought most fully to bear. Most of her judges were graduates and members of the faculty of the University of Paris. Obviously they began the trial prejudiced against her. The chief charge brought against her was that of being an unsubmissive heretic, although the record (which may have been doctored) is pocked with minor, oft-repeated charges: theft of the bishop's horse; "her hair cut round above her ears"; "nothing about her to display and announce her sex, save Nature's own distinctive marks."

On the first day of the judicial proceedings, which were to last over three months, Joan courageously refused to accept the bishop's command that she not, under penalty of conviction of heresy, leave her prison without authorization. She declared that she would not accept his prohibition, adding that if she escaped, none could accuse her of breaking her oath, since she had not taken one. More than three centuries before the Fifth Amendment, Joan was invoking its spirit: When asked by her judges if it had been revealed to her that she would escape, she countered, "That is not in your case. Do you want me to speak against myself?"

Joan had a natural ease in a courtroom. (In fact, this trial was not her first experience with the law: earlier, she had defended herself successfully in a breach-of-promise suit.) Now, at this far graver trial, her judges were not able to shake her confidence or her spirit. She was asked whether the voice of St. Margaret spoke to her in English. "Why should she speak English? She is not on the English side," was her answer. To the question was St. Michael naked when he appeared to her she answered, "Do you think God has not wherewithal to clothe him?"

The English got the sentence they wanted; Joan was decreed a heretic and abandoned "to the secular justice as a limb of Satan, infected with the leprosy of heresy, cut off from the Church, in order to prevent the infection of the other members of Christ." "Justice," secular and ecclesiastical, succeeded in having Joan burned at the stake.

In burning her at the stake, her executioner may have thought he did his job professionally and well and that the world had heard the last of her. Such has not been the case.

An American historian writing in the seventies argued, "Our principles and ideals have been so loftily elevated that we have often been unable to live by them consistently or realize even an approximation of them." The beauty of Joan of Arc is that her principles and ideals were so simply presented that she does not frighten off the rest of us from the hope of realizing an approximation of them. This is part of what gives her an eternal quality.

She is a woman for today. Her problems could be our problems, albeit less dramatic. She belonged to a minority. Her civil liberties were disregarded. She refused to be locked into conformity. She tussled with supremacy of conscience long before Vatican Council II courageously took a new look at the primacy of the individual conscience when well formed.

In all that Joan of Arc did, she had an abiding awareness of God's help, and total trust in Him. This is her most important message. It is why she was able to "go boldly."

# Thomas More

## (1478–1535)

### DAN HERR

*The son of John More, a lawyer and judge, Thomas More was born in London on February 7. He became a page in the household of Archbishop John Morton at Canterbury when about twelve, went to Oxford, studied law at Lincoln's Inn, and was admitted to the bar in 1501 and entered Parliament in 1504. He thought of becoming a Carthusian, decided against it, and in 1505 married Jane Colt. Their home became a center of learning and medieval and renaissance thought in England. More became one of the leading figures of his time, noted for his ability, intellect, and wit. He wrote poetry, history, treatises against Protestantism, and prayers, and translated Lucian from the Latin. His* Vindication of Henry Against Luther, *in 1523, was a spirited defense of King Henry VIII, and his* Utopia *(1515–16), an account of an imaginary society ruled by reason, has become a classic.*

*He tutored young Henry VIII, became an undersheriff in London in 1510, and the following year married a widow, Alice Middleton, a month after his first wife's death. When Henry became king, he sent More on several diplomatic missions in France and Flanders, appointed him to the Royal*

*Council in 1517, and knighted him in 1521. He became chancellor, succeeding Cardinal Wolsey in 1529, despite grave misgivings about Henry's action in defying the Pope by seeking to divorce Catherine of Aragon. He refused to have any part in the discussion regarding the king's divorce and angered Henry by refusing to sign the request to the Pope to permit Henry to dismiss Catherine. After opposing a series of measures against the Church, he resigned the chancellorship in 1532 and retired to his home in Chelsea. When he would not take the oath, provided in the Act of Succession, recognizing the offspring of Henry and his second wife, Anne Boleyn, as heir to the throne, declaring Henry's first marriage to Catherine was no true marriage and repudiating the Pope, he was imprisoned in the Tower of London in 1534. He maintained silence when Cromwell asked him to comment on the Act of Supremacy the following year and was accused of treason. Despite his continued refusal to speak on the Act he was convicted of treason. On July 6 he was beheaded, proclaiming, as he mounted the scaffold, that he was "the King's good servant but God's first." He was canonized in 1935. His feast day is celebrated on June 22.*

Almost everyone would agree that leaders and heroes are in short supply these days. Not only in America but throughout the world, we suffer from a lack of inspiring leaders. With envy as well as nostalgia we recall the days of FDR, John and Robert Kennedy, Martin Luther King, Charles de Gaulle, and Winston Churchill. And we feel sorry for our kids, who have no heroes to live up to as we did when we were young. If we are questioned on our contemporary heroes, we are embarrassed by our fumbling efforts to name someone in the heroic mold.

Possibly the same spirit that makes us reluctant to create new heroes in our day is also responsible for the way we have downgraded our saints. Saints just aren't what they used to be in American Catholic life. Ever since the Vatican announced that Saint Philomena never existed and that the reality of good old Saint Christopher was as questionable, saints seem to have faded from the contemporary religious scene. Catholic bookstores, which at one time had whole sections devoted to hagiography—mostly poorly written tomes that embalmed their subjects in treacle—now have difficulty coming up with a handful of books about the saints for the rare customer who is still interested in the subject. The liturgists (who, in my opinion, have much to answer for on a variety of fronts) helped denigrate the saints when they perpetrated a de-emphasis of feast days in the liturgy. This treason was followed by the elimination of saints' days from Catholic calendars, and before we realized what had happened, most saints had disappeared over the horizon.

Two saints, other than the Blessed Virgin, who *have* survived the blight are Francis of Assisi and Thomas More, both of whom have through the years managed to appeal to the widest variety of people. Thomas More's reputation may well have been helped by Robert Bolt, the English dramatist whose glorious *A Man for All Seasons* was a successful play and movie. For many it was an introduction to Thomas More, and most viewers liked what they saw. Possibly the most interesting aspect of Thomas More's current popularity is that he has been embraced by both liberals and conservatives, as well as by those who occupy the center of the political and religious spectrum. Surprisingly, the final testing of Thomas More has had various meanings for various people, and as a result, his life is used as an argument to buttress conflicting philosophies. Thomas More himself, I suggest, would be delighted to learn that he may have become all things to all men—he, of all people.

The facts about Thomas More are readily available. Thanks to his own books and letters and to the writings of his admiring son-in-law, as well as letters of the great humanist Erasmus, we know far more about More than about most saints. (The only thing we don't know, despite the well-publicized presence of alleged relics, is what happened to his body.) More was born in London in 1478. An able lawyer, he rose rapidly through the monarchistic political tangle of six-teenth-century England to become Henry VIII's Lord Chancellor in 1529; a scholar, linguist, translator, and author (known principally for *Utopia*, a speculative essay about an imaginary island that embodies More's considerations on the perfect political system), he was friend to and correspondent of some of the most learned and enlightened minds in Europe; he refused to sanction the king's second marriage (to Anne Boleyn), resigned his chancellorship, and forfeited his fortune and, in 1535, his life; he was canonized in 1935.

To understand Thomas More and to appreciate what his life can mean to us four and a half centuries later, we need to add more color to these bare facts.

Raised under the tutelage of John Morton, Cardinal Archbishop of Canterbury, and educated at Oxford, the gifted young More was strongly attracted to the scholarly life. In obedience to his father, he took up an active life in law, at which he quickly distinguished himself. But he never ceased to be a student of the classics and of the Fathers of the Church, and the more he studied, the stronger grew his inclination to become a monk. He went so far as to live as a sort of guest in a Carthusian monastery for several years, practicing his law by day and returning to the monastery and following the monastic life as he could. It was a sensible way—typical of him—to test the possibility of a religious vocation, which he finally decided against in favor of marriage. He concluded, as Erasmus tells us, that for him it would be better "to be a chaste husband than a priest impure."

He married Jane Colt, who bore him four children in as many years (Margaret, Elizabeth, Cecily, and John) and died shortly after bearing a stillborn fifth child, in the sixth year of their marriage. With four small children to raise, Thomas More did not delay long in remarrying, choosing Alice Middleton, a widow considerably older than himself, of whom, in an uncharacteristically ungallant moment, he once said, "She is neither a pearl nor a girl." But sharp-tongued Dame Alice was, if reports are reliable, quite able to take care of herself ("aged, blunt, and crude," Erasmus described her). She took good care of her household, too, and proved a suitable, if somewhat austere, stepmother to the children.

The More household at Chelsea, alongside the Thames, before the trouble with King Henry, has been celebrated as sort of a Christianized version of Plato's Academy set down in a bedlam. There were always people underfoot, much activity, much conversation, much studying, much laughter, and much love. More said he believed in being "merrie, jocunde, and pleasaunte" at home. In spite of his high position and its prerogatives, the Lord Chancellor was not attracted by life at court.

Through his law practice, his royal appointment, and his scholarly reputation, Thomas More developed a wide circle of friends both great and humble. Evidently, a magnetic and charming personality was matched with one of the best brains of the century. Few men in history have been the subject of so many unsolicited testimonials, of which this one by Whittinton, a fellow scholar, is characteristic (and gave Robert Bolt the title for his play): "More is a man of an angel's wit and singular learning. I know not his fellow. For where is the man of that gentleness, lowliness, and affability? And, as the time requireth, a man of marvelous mirth and pastimes, and sometimes of as sad gravity. A man for all seasons."

As so often happens in life, when everything seemed to be going well for More the seeds of destruction that were sowed when he accepted Henry's appointment as Lord Chancellor of England flowered into tragedy. In the complex series of events in which Henry VIII moved from his proud position as Defender of the Faith to head of the Church in England, put away his first wife, and married Anne Boleyn, there were many intermediate steps. Thomas More was a good lawyer, and he knew his way around the inside of an oath. He had no objection, for instance, to making public recognition that any heirs of the king's second marriage should be the rightful successors to the English throne. The king and parliament had the right to name whomever they wished to rule. Thomas More said as much, leaving unspoken the rest of the sentence: *even though they be illegitimate.*

Nor did Thomas More, after he had resigned his chancellorship, feel compelled to go about making public denunciation of the king's action—a course that not only would have been rashly suicidal but questionable conduct on the part of a former member of the government. Yet, to the king and to many other Englishmen, More's silence shouted louder than the fervent approval of a thousand lesser men, and Henry could not be content until, one way or another, he extracted public approval from Thomas More of the marriage to Anne and an acknowledgment that Henry was the supreme head of the Church in England.

And it was at this point that Thomas More felt his back to be up against the wall of his own conscience. The wall was invisible to the world, but it was nonetheless real to Thomas More. Here the gracious scholar who loved life, family, and friends became a man apart, listening to but one voice. His family implored him—for his sake and for theirs—to take the oath (and indeed his stand entailed ruin for his family); his daughter Margaret, of whom he was especially fond, persuaded herself that she could take the oath and did, hoping to sway her father to do the same; it is probable that the king himself did not want to execute Thomas More if it could be avoided, but there was that essential matter of the need for More's approval, and there was no turning back.

Thomas More sat with his conscience for fifteen lonely months in the Tower of London, in poor health, isolated from the other prisoners, forbidden his beloved books, deprived finally of even pen and paper. But neither his conscience nor his writing hand lagged. He scrawled last messages to his family with charcoal ("Farewell, my dear child, and pray for me and I shall for you and all your friends that we may merrily meet in heaven") and went to his death proclaiming that he died "the King's good servant, but God's first."

What makes Thomas More a man to be admired and emulated in our age—an age that knows few heroes? So he was an intellectual, a nice guy ("the most good-natured of men," according to Erasmus), a man of courage, a loving father, a good husband, and a loyal friend. But fortunately for civilization, he was not unique in these distinctions. And others have suffered as much as Thomas More, dared as much, loved God as much. I submit that More stands out among the heroes and martyrs and saints of history because he is a man to whom twentieth-century Americans can relate.

Like us, Thomas More lived in a transitional era, a time when the old system was breaking up and the complexion of the new was yet to be determined. In his day there was the revolution of the printing press and the discovery of the New World; in our day, television and landing on the moon. In both times the laity became restive over clerical domination of their Church. The sixteenth (like the twentieth) century saw the rise of reformers and a defensive and frequently irrational reaction on the part of the Church as these reformers struck where the Church was most vulnerable. His was a time, as is ours, when sincere men might disagree on the solution to vital problems affecting the Church and the world, when faith becomes increasingly elusive and when hope is difficult to sustain.

I suggest that Thomas More can speak to us across the centuries because he embodied qualities that today we admire and envy. Some readers may consider me frivolous when I begin by emphasizing More's delightful sense of humor. Certainly if we can believe hagiographers, saints and a sense of humor are seldom found together (as Phyllis McGinley writes: "Some saints are alien . . . hard to love"). Admittedly I am not an authority, but I know of no other saint whose wit is at least equal to his sanctity. Evident in much of what he wrote or said, it did not even fail him on the scaffold. To a guard he said, "I pray thee see me safe up, and for my coming down let me shift for myself." And he is supposed to have asked his executioner to take care not to cut his beard with the ax since it, at least, was innocent of treason. Anyone who can joke at a time like that shows radical signs of being an unusually human sort of saint.

And being a "human sort of saint" is precisely why Thomas More speaks to us from across four and a half centuries. He lived in an age of extremists and fanatics yet resolutely resisted the temptation to lose his balance. He hewed to the middle of the road, a position no more popular then than today. He hated and denounced the new "heresies" but permitted his son-in-law, Daniel Roper, a convert to Lutheranism who "did abhor" his father-in-law, to live under his roof for many years, a source of personal and official embarrassment for More. Again, Thomas More was far from happy with the views of the radical reformers of his day—although he did not deny the critical problems facing the Church—but he continued to enjoy an intimate and fruitful friendship with the greatest of the radical reformers, Erasmus, whom Pope Paul IV branded as "the leader of all heretics." (This friendship must have been a juicy item for the devil's advocate when More's cause was being scrutinized.)

The memory of Thomas More was recalled by many of us, I think, during the Watergate days, when no one in government seemed free from the taint of corruption. We remembered the attempts of unprincipled sixteenth-century English politicians (the Nixons, Ehrlichmans, and Haldemans of the day) to entrap More and how he resisted and outwitted them, so that despite their conspiratorial efforts, no smear could befoul him.

Thomas More was a man of peace, of tranquillity, of reason. And yet when it seemed to him that he must take a stand, that his conscience demanded the ultimate sacrifice, he did not hesitate. As the character the Common Man reminds us at the end of Bolt's *A Man for All Seasons*, "It isn't difficult to keep alive, friends—just don't make trouble." We, too, can save ourselves with a word, a small compromise from time to time, a momentary closing of the eyes, a plugging of the interior ear, a barely discernible shrug of the shoulders. There was never a time when it was easier to bury the body of a murdered conscience without risk of detection. Saint Thomas More kept his conscience alive at the cost of his own life. His prayer in the Tower of London must be our prayer today: "Give me Thy grace, good Lord, to set the world at nought. . . ."

# Ignatius Loyola

## (1491–1556)

### JOHN B. BRESLIN, S.J.

Of a noble family and the son of Don Betrán Yáñez de
Loyola and Marina Saenz de Licona y Balda, Ignatius (christened Íñigo) was born in the family castle in Guipúzcoa,
Spain, the youngest of thirteen children. He entered the military service of the Duke of Nájera and was wounded in the
right leg during the siege of Pamplona in 1521. While recu-
perating he was so impressed by a life of Christ and biographies of the saints he read that he decided to devote himself
to Christ. After he recovered he went on a pilgrimage to
Montserrat, where he hung up his sword at our Lord's altar.
He spent a year, in 1522–23, on retreat at Manresa, where he
experienced visions and probably wrote the bulk of his Spiritual Exercises (which was not published until 1548). From
1524 to 1535 he studied at Barcelona, Alcalá, Salamanca
(where he was accused and then exonerated of heresy for his
preaching), and Paris. He received his master's degree in
1534, when he was forty-three, and in the same year in Paris,
with six fellow students, founded the Jesuits, though the formal name, Society of Jesus, was not adopted until 1537,
when Ignatius was ordained in Venice after a year's pilgrim-

*age through Spain. Unable to go on pilgrimage to Jerusalem, as they had wanted, they went to Rome and offered their services to the Pope. It was while on the way to Rome that Ignatius had the famous vision of La Storta, in which Christ promised all would go well in Rome. The order was approved by Pope Paul III in 1540 and the group took their final vows in 1541 with Ignatius as superior-general. Jesuits were sent at once to missionary areas, and soon Jesuit schools, colleges, and seminaries spread all over Europe as the Jesuits became noted for their prowess in the field of education. By the time of Ignatius' death, in Rome on July 31, Ignatius' three goals for the Jesuits—reform of the Church, especially by education and more frequent use of the sacraments; missionary activities; and the fight against heresy—were well established as the basis of Jesuit activities. He was canonized in 1622.*

Dorothy Day does not like it when people call her a saint. More than humility, true or false, is involved in that reaction, for, as she has shrewdly observed, the tag "saint" allows us to honor the person without having to hear her message. Admiration, not imitation, is our classic response. In his final years, as he guided his infant society from headquarters in Rome, Ignatius Loyola had something of the same problem. "Il Santo," his enthusiastic young followers would call him—but never to his face. Hagiographers have not felt hampered by such considerations; other writers, however—and not a few distinguished ones—have paid Ignatius the dubious compliment of considering him as much a knave as a saint.

In this he would seem the direct antithesis of that other great founder, Francis of Assisi, Christianity's most universally popular saint. The calculating soldier-saint of Loyola, with his mechanical "exercises" for attaining devotion and his *Realpolitik* machinations for gaining power in Church and world, and the gentle lover of nature from Assisi, with his paeans to sun and water and his devotion to Lady Poverty—thus have they come down to us, and is it any wonder that

statues of Francis far outsell those of Ignatius? I don't want
to play the game of historical revisionism, but I do think that
on the theological level—where the sanctity of the two men
has meaning for all Christians and not just for their respec-
tive orders—the religious experiences of Francis and Ignatius
have much in common. And I trust that my Franciscan
brethren will pardon me for borrowing a few details from the
life of their founder to illustrate my point.

It's interesting to recall that at one point in his youth
Francis wanted nothing better than to be a soldier, riding off
to fight in the Crusades, and much later, he managed to get
himself attached to a group of crusaders in Egypt in a burst
of missionary zeal. More important for our purpose than this
military affinity between Francis and Ignatius is their experience of conversion. Both left their families to give themselves
over to solitary prayer and, coincidentally, both found their
"deserts" in caves. No more illuminating explanation of what
happened to each of them can be found, I think, than G. K.
Chesterton's interpretation of Francis' "dark night":

> Francis, at the time or somewhere about the time when
> he disappeared into the prison or the dark cavern, under-
> went a reversal of a certain psychological kind; which
> was really like the reversal of a complete somersault, in
> that by coming full circle it came back, or apparently
> came back, to the same normal posture. . . . He looked
> on the world as differently from other men as if he had
> come out of that dark hole walking on his hands. . . .

> This state can only be represented in symbol; but the
> symbol of inversion is true in another way. If a man saw
> the world upside down, with all the trees and flowers
> hanging head downwards as in a pool, one effect would
> be to emphasise the idea of *dependence*. . . . Being in
> some mystical sense on the other side of things, he sees
> things go forth from the divine as children going forth
> from a familiar and accepted home, instead of meeting
> them as they come out, as most of us do, upon the roads
> of the world. And it is the paradox that by this privilege

he is more familiar, more free and fraternal, more carelessly hospitable than we.

Chesterton, of course, has taken certain literary liberties with Francis' cave, but the insight he conveys goes far beyond a rhetorical flourish. In fact, it expresses in symbolic terms the core mystical experience of both Francis and Ignatius that makes them brothers in the Christian tradition.

In recent years the eminent German theologians Hugo and Karl Rahner have shown in a series of essays what it is that characterizes Ignatian spirituality. Put most simply—though the insight is by no means easy to appropriate—the experience Ignatius underwent during his "novitiate" at Manresa was exactly the kind of radical transformation that Chesterton describes. It was as if the world has been turned upside down or inside out: everything was the same and yet completely different. Ignatius now saw and found God in everything—not by force of will or by a trick of the imagination but simply because his prayer had led him to see the world, as he put it, "from above." Words and images begin to break down here, for what we are trying to describe is, in the literal sense, a transcendent experience: the world seen now as if from God's point of view, where everything becomes transparent, everything is known experientially as Christians acknowledge it to be ontologically, i.e., wholly dependent on the Creator and Lord.

A hard saying for children of a secular age but nothing very startling in the history of mysticism, West or East. What makes Ignatius' contribution exceptional is the link he saw and developed between this grace of immersion in the Godhead and the apostolic calling of every Christian to be at work here below redeeming the time. The link was Christ, for in Him the "above" has graciously come down to live in our midst. Ignatius himself could not have picked a better New Testament text to illustrate this mysterious commerce of above and below than the verses from the second chapter of Paul's letter to the Philippians, which the Church chose as the Entrance Song for his feast:

> Have this mind among yourselves, which you have in Christ Jesus, who, though he was in the form of God, did not count equality with God a thing to be grasped, but emptied himself, taking the form of a servant, being born in the likeness of men. And being found in human form he humbled himself and became obedient unto death, even death on a cross. Therefore God has highly exalted him and bestowed on him the name which is above every name, that at the name of Jesus every knee should bow, in heaven and on earth and under the earth, and every tongue confess that Jesus Christ is Lord, to the glory of God the Father.

Just as the "therefore" is the key to the theology of this early Christian hymn, so, too, is it the linchpin of Ignatius' personal spirituality and that of his *Spiritual Exercises*. As God in Christ freely gave up all claim to divine prerogatives in order to become the One Mediator between the "above" and the "below" by entering fully into human experience, and that at its most painful, and only thus re-entered the glory of His Father, so everyone who wishes to experience the fullness of God's life must follow the same path that Jesus walked.

Again, there is nothing particularly startling about that Christological insight, for as the Pauline hymn indicates, it was part of the earliest self-understanding of the Church. What makes Ignatius extraordinary is the manner in which he discovered that principle for himself and, even more, his ability to translate it into a doctrine of prayer and a way of life.

At Manresa, and most dramatically during the intellectual vision on the banks of the Cardoner River, Ignatius proved upon his pulses, in Keats's phrase, the truth of that Christological doctrine. He experienced in a way that left no doubt in his mind the fundamental truths of faith, so that he could say in his *Autobiography*, dictated late in life in the third person: "The things he saw strengthened him then and always gave him such strength in his faith that he often thought to himself: if there were no Scriptures to teach us these matters of the faith, he would be resolved to die for them, only because of what he had seen." The vision or, more properly, illumination was a pure gift of grace, but it came only after Ignatius had surrendered himself completely to God, gradually stripping off layer after layer of egoism and self-love, a process that began during his recuperation at Loyola from the wound suffered at Pamplona and continued, at a price of great suffering, all through his time at Manresa. The cost of discipleship for Ignatius included periods of such intense scrupulosity and subsequent depression that he seriously considered suicide.

Letting go of himself, in imitation of Christ, who poured Himself out, was the price Ignatius paid for his entry into the "above." But what he discovered—and this was to be the hallmark of his spiritual doctrine—was that his mystical experience, far from drawing him away from the world Christ had entered and transformed, sent him back with a totally new vision that allowed him to find God in all things. As Pedro de Ribadeneira, Ignatius' first biographer, put it: "We often saw how even the smallest things could make his spirit soar upwards to God, who even in the smallest things is Greatest. At the sight of a little plant, a leaf, a flower or a fruit, an insignificant worm or a tiny animal Ignatius could soar free above the heavens and reach through into things which lie beyond the senses."

This is not, properly speaking, nature mysticism, for the movement is principally downward rather than upward. Because he had been granted a comprehensive vision of the universe in its intimate relation to its Creator and Lord, a favorite Ignatian expression, Ignatius "saw through" nature to the divine reality it both revealed and concealed, much the way, as Chesterton would have it, that Francis emerged from his cave with a vision of all creatures literally dependent on God, suspended by grace rather than firmly planted in a world of their own making.

Francis expressed his insight in more lyrical form in his *Canticle* and other poems, but Ignatius had as profound a regard for the senses and built his contemplations in the *Spiritual Exercises* around the sounds, sights, even smells of the Gospels. At the end of the day's exercises, Ignatius specifically recommends what he calls an "application of the senses," a repetition of the day's contemplation that focuses precisely on the sensible particulars in the scene. The emphasis here, as throughout the *Exercises*, is on entering into the mystery rather than simply thinking about it; but by insisting on the use of the senses, Ignatius reveals the degree to which he takes the Incarnation literally. If leaves or worms could send him into mystical ecstasy, it is no wonder that details from the gospel scenes offered even greater opportunities for consolation, for the link between Jesus the Word and the Word of the Scriptures was a highly developed theme in medieval theology. Just as he arrived at his periods of divine illumination after a long period of wrestling with the realities of his own life and, in particular, his sense of sinfulness, so the sights and sounds, the taste and feel of everyday reality, and especially the commonplace facts of the gospel narratives, purged of all bias toward sin, remained for Ignatius the surest and most direct avenue to renewed contact with his Creator and Lord.

According to Hugo Rahner, Ignatius perceived that this dialectic unity between the above and the below, between grace and nature, was effected not by dissolving one into the other, much less by abandoning one pole of the tension, but only through the person of Christ. He stands in the middle, uniting the divine and the human, unconfusedly and undividedly. Rahner sees this insight as the unifying thread throughout the *Exercises* and, indeed, in all of Ignatius' writings. It certainly helps explain some of the paradoxes associated with Ignatius' life and thought.

For example, the well-known maxim about trusting in God

and at the same time working vigorously ourselves (which dates, incidentally, from the early-eighteenth century) takes on new meaning when we realize how its commonly understood form is really an inversion of its original wording, a rewriting occasioned by a desire to make the principle reflect a logical rather than a Christological insight. It usually runs something like this: Trust in God as if success depended wholly on Him, not on yourself; work as if you were doing everything and God nothing. In fact, the first version was the exact opposite of that: Trust in God as if success depended wholly on you, not on God; work as if God alone was doing everything and you nothing. It's easy to see why it was transformed, for at first blush the original seems rather shocking, perhaps even absurd. But recent commentators, notably another distinguished Jesuit theologian, Gustave Martelet, have shown how it expresses in fact the very insight we have seen. The first half reminds us that our faith in God is not a substitute for the need to co-operate with grace (against fideism), and the second warns us against the dangers of Pelagianism by insisting that ultimately it is God who brings all of our works to perfection, not ourselves. The balance here is much subtler than in the "rationalized" version and, to that degree, truer to Ignatius' understanding of the correct relation between the above and the below, between the infinite majesty of God and His divine condescension in Christ.

It is precisely this point that the standard caricatures of Ignatius miss. His was no bootstrap spirituality, no early model of "muscular Christianity." He knew his Augustine, but even more, he had learned at Manresa how dependent he was on God's initiative and how stupendously generous God was in pouring out His grace.

A terse Latin aphorism attributed to an unknown Flemish Jesuit catches the spirit neatly: *Non coerceri maximo, contineri tamen a minimo divinum est* ([God] suffers under no compulsion, no matter how great, and yet He can be contained by the smallest of created things). In both maxims, it is Ignatius' sense of freedom that shines forth, that liberating power which flows from a total awareness of our dependence on a God whose very nature it is to give freely of Himself. No coercion of any kind; complete self-surrender before the Father's love. What better summary of Christ's own life? What better program for one who wished to give his own life in service to Christ's Church?

Freedom and service. Those two ideals, never to be separated, form the basis of Ignatian spirituality, and they echo, in another key, all the pairs we have already seen as dialectical partners in Ignatius' highly personal yet profoundly traditional theology: the above and the below; the divine and the human; nature and grace. They also explain why the *Spiritual Exercises,* removed from the preacher's hands and returned to the original forum of retreatant and director, have flowered once again in our day as a way of prayer and of Christian decision. Freedom and service speak directly to the personal and, indeed, the political crises of our time. The world-wide clamor for human rights rises from men and women who want to be free and to have their freedom respected. It rises as well in places where political liberty is assured but where economic, social, or psychological fetters remain firmly in place. The service demanded is a ministry that recognizes the genuine need for bread yet recognizes, too, that bread alone will never be sufficient. Only a servant who is free of self-serving motives and of ideology can perform such a ministry, and it is toward the attainment of such freedom that Ignatius' *Exercises* and his *Constitutions* for his new society are aimed.

In this light, several striking features of those *Constitutions* become much clearer. As a novice, I remember listening to lengthy explanations of the society's rules and being struck by the number of times Ignatius would introduce the phrase "in our Lord" after such a verb as "think" or "consider" or "judge." Similarly, even the most pragmatic prescriptions for the ordering of life in the society would be punctuated by references to "the greater glory of God" or

"the service of the Divine Majesty." At first this all seemed
merely a pious reflex, like ritual genuflections in church. But
gradually I began to realize that those phrases were the heart
of Ignatius' message to his sons and that everything else—all
the prudent safeguards against tyranny or anarchy—were sec-
ondary, at least for the author. He believed completely in
"the interior law of charity and love which the Holy Spirit
writes and engraves upon hearts" and which, far more than
any external legislation, would keep the society alive and
flourishing. It was, as we have seen, this very "interior law"
that Ignatius learned at Manresa and that remained for the
rest of his life the foundation upon which he built his own
spirituality and that of his companions. Here again we find
"the above," from which all else flowed. But Ignatius knew,
too, "the below" and put into practice the principle that
trust in God requires our co-operation—and so he set about
drawing up his "external law," the *Constitutions*. And yet he
constantly returned to the fundamental point and converted
it into a motif (*in Domino nostro*) that continually breaks
through the canonical language of the rules.

Even more explicit is a one-page summary of Ignatius' attitude toward natural gifts, included as an appendix to an early
draft of the *Constitutions*. Using classical theological terms,
Ignatius lists a hierarchy of divine gifts ranging from sanctifying grace through actual graces to natural gifts. The first class
is always to be preferred, for it directly concerns an individual's relationship to God. But, in the interests of the apostolate—the goal of service, once again—Ignatius remarks that,
other things being equal, "the one possessing these natural
gifts will be a better instrument for the universal and spiritual good of souls than the other who is not provided with
them." At the same time, in a labored passage that is so characteristic of Ignatius' personal style, he reminds us that just
as we are deceived if we think we can receive "the graces and
spiritual gifts of the first class" without preparing ourselves
(one thinks of his desert experience at Manresa) or if we neg-
lect to use our natural gifts when they are united with God's

free grace, so, too, we run a serious risk if we seek those natural gifts "without being possessed or adorned by the graces of the first set, because it is much worse and more dangerous to possess these gifts . . . when we do not profit from those of the first [set], since those of the first set are in their entirety intended to unite us in true love with the Divine Goodness."

For all the syntactic contortions of this passage, its message is by now quite familiar and straightforward: the above and the below must never be separated, but, in any given circumstance, if one is forced to choose, those graces that unite the individual to God always take precedence. Indeed, Ignatius goes so far as to warn against seeking to develop natural talents apart from God, for their very goodness can become a trap. "Lilies that fester smell far worse than weeds," Shakespeare tells us, in a rather different context; on that point he and Ignatius would agree. Ignatius could be equally ruthless, however, about the graces of the second set, including the mystical gifts with which he was so richly endowed. Several times in his life, especially during his studies, he recognized that the overwhelming consolations he experienced were really a temptation, since they distracted him from the more important, if considerably more mundane, business of educating himself for his future work as an apostle. Similarly, in his later years he learned from his doctor that the gift of tears was threatening his eyesight and hence his usefulness to the society. Poised between freedom and service, desiring only the advancement of the Kingdom, Ignatius could forgo this mystical gift in favor of continued work. It is worth noting, to conclude where we began, Karl Rahner's observation that "Saint Francis had angrily rejected precisely the same remonstrances of the physician."

The Ignatius revealed by these texts casts quite a different shadow from the figure of popular legend. He enjoyed a degree of mystical experience, and often sensible consolation, that puts him in a very special class of Christian saints, with Teresa of Ávila and John of the Cross, for example. And despite his unpoetic nature, his writings have succeeded in communicating the fruits of that experience to tens of thousands of disciples, in and out of the Society of Jesus, for more than four hundred years. The Jesuit vocation was once aptly described by a colleague of mine as "being a monk in Times Square." At times, the Society of Jesus has stressed one half of that polarity to the detriment of the other. Not too long ago, the monastic model held sway; more recently, at least in the United States, identification with the *Zeitgeist* has captured the imagination of many Jesuits. But, as we have seen, Ignatius always strove to keep his dialectical pairs (above and below, grace and nature, freedom and service) in a healthy tension. Even for so great a mystic and saint, that was not always easy. It is no wonder, then, that his sons often have trouble duplicating his balancing act. But the challenge remains, and when it is met, as Ignatius himself met it, one can only stand in awe, with Gerard Manley Hopkins, before "the achieve of, the mastery of the thing!"

# Teresa of Ávila

## (1515–82)

### MARY PURCELL

*One of the most profound mystics of all times, Teresa was born on March 28 in Ávila, Spain, the daughter of Alonso Sánchez de Cepeda and his second wife, Beatrice Davila y Ahumada. She was one of nine children of this marriage (and three from Alonso's first marriage) and was early attracted to the religious life. She became a Carmelite at Ávila in 1536, was professed the next year, left because of serious illness in 1538, but returned two years later. She experienced visions and heard voices, which caused her great difficulty in her spiritual life until Peter of Alcantara became her spiritual adviser and convinced her these experiences were authentic.*

*Despite bitter opposition, she founded St. Joseph of Ávila monastery in 1562 for nuns wishing to live an austere, enclosed spiritual life, as contrasted with the lax atmosphere so prevalent in convents of that time. In 1567, Father Rubeo, prior general of the Carmelites, gave her permission to establish other convents based on the strict rules of St. Joseph's, and she eventually established sixteen convents. While setting up a convent at Medino del Campo, she met John of the Cross, founded her first monastery (the first reform monas-*

tery) for men, at Duruelo in 1568, and then turned the task
of founding men's monasteries for the reform movement over
to John. She was tireless in her efforts to reform the Carmelites, and in 1572 Father Rubeo put strict restrictions on
her reforming group. During the next few years, a bitter
struggle raged between the reformers and the nonreformers,
until in 1580 Pope Gregory XIII, at the instigation of King
Philip II of Spain, recognized the Discalced Reform as a separate province.

During these turbulent years, Teresa traveled all over Spain
and wrote numerous letters and books which are widely recognized as classics of spiritual literature, among them her Autobiography (1565), Way of Perfection (1573), and Interior
Castle (1577). Intelligent, charming, forceful, as have few
others she successfully united a highly active life with a life
of deep contemplation. She died in Alba de Tormes, Spain,
was canonized by Pope Gregory XV in 1622, and was declared a Doctor of the Church by Pope Paul VI in 1970, the
first woman to be so honored. Though she died on October
4, her feast day is celebrated on October 15, as the Gregorian
calendar went into effect the day after her death, suppressing
the next ten days.


When I think of Teresa, my favorite woman saint, I find myself wondering why I feel so akin to her. Her childhood and
mine had at least one common factor in that we both learned
to read at a very early age. And we both had mothers who
were themselves avid readers and who encouraged us to read;
but, though they allowed us to read much that was trivial,
they also helped us to acquire a taste for spiritual reading,
even in childhood.

In later life, when I became interested in history, the re-
semblances between the passing pageant of Teresa's times
and mine struck me as quite remarkable. The Renaissance,
on the upsurge at her birth, in 1515, had come to full tide
before her death, sixty-seven years later. I see her, silhouetted

against her splendid century, with its plethora of poets, artists, men of action and men of vision, flamboyant princes, rulers whose power was absolute and whose word was law, great sinners and great saints. Similar characters are not wanting today.

The discoveries of new territories in the sixteenth century have their counterpart in modern space exploration. Then, as now, there were new sciences, new technologies, new forms of art and literature, and a vast expansion of human knowledge. Teresa's life, like mine, was lived in a transitional, turbulent period of human history, a period when the old order changed and vanished, yielding place to the new; vast wealth existed side by side with a world of have-nots; intrepid courage and selfless charity flourished, as did injustice, cruelty, and man's inhumanity to man. The widely held, if purblind, conviction that to man all things are possible, the wavering and diminishing belief in God and the afterlife, were characteristics of Teresa's time, as they are of ours. I can imagine her pondering, as I sometimes do, Christ's plaintive question: *When the Son of Man comes, will he find faith on earth?*

In her lifetime the power of the printed word to influence people's ideas and decisions had been realized. Masses who had mastered the technique of reading without having learned to assess the full meaning, the worth, the truth of what they read were easily swayed—because of their vulnerability—this way and that. So my saint knows the apprehensions that grip us when we see power slip from rulers— even from rulers elected by us, the people—to those who through the media can mastermind the thinking and actions of millions.

Teresa would understand the difficulties of some Catholics and the enthusiasm of others in this post-Council period, for she lived through just such a transitional period; she was a senior citizen at a time when the Church was a Church in a hurry. She accepted change, realizing that it was as necessary as it was belated. She may have sighed when some pious customs dating from medieval times were relinquished; so she

knows how I felt in Dublin the evening I saw in our streets
for the last time the snowy-white cornets of the Sisters of
Charity, being discarded next day for less quaint, more utili-
tarian headgear. She knows how Catholics whose religious
formation dated from the pre-1960 decades felt when cata-
pulted into the speedy-change era following Vatican II; in
1560, as in 1960, the Church had to accelerate and adapt to
keep up with the secular world, forging ahead at ever-increas-
ing tempo; that world had to be overtaken if the mission of
preaching the gospel to all was to be fulfilled.

I cannot remember when I first read Teresa's writings; it
was certainly many years ago. Although the *Life, The Way of
Perfection,* and *The Interior Castle,* spiritual classics, were far
beyond my comprehension, I found them strangely attractive.
I still cannot follow her to those lofty heights, the climate so
congenial to her spirit, but on the lower reaches there are
hundreds of helps for lesser mortals. The fact that she dallied
long, before finally committing herself wholly to the call *Be
perfect, as your heavenly Father is perfect,* is consoling and
encouraging to those of us whose conversions are at best half-
hearted compromises. I find this wise observation of hers
helpful:

> One should not wait until one is perfect, or even until
> one is converted before giving oneself to prayer. . . . It
> would be the sad day if we could not draw near to God
> until we were dead to worldly things. Think of the
> Magdalen and the Samaritan woman and the woman of
> Canaan. Were they perfect or converted when they
> approached and found him?

I find chapters 27 to 42 in *The Way of Perfection,* her
treatise on that prayer of everyman, the *Our Father,* a great
help. She rises to magnificent heights describing the universal
prayer bequeathed to mankind by Christ; she stresses its
uniqueness, which permits the person saying it to adapt it to
suit himself:

> In its few words are enshrined all contemplation and all

perfection. If we study it, no other book seems necessary. In it Our Lord teaches us to pray, the whole method from the beginnings of mental prayer to the Prayer of Quiet and Union. It would be a good thing for us to consider that he has taught this prayer to each one of us individually and is continually teaching it to us. . . . He meant it as a general prayer for the use of all; everyone could interpret it as he thought right, ask for what he wants and find comfort in doing so.

Readers unfamiliar with the saint's writings should begin with *The Book of the Foundations*, which might also be entitled *A Traveler in Sixteenth-century Spain*. Teresa wrote it to let her nuns know how her reform work and the founding of new Carmels was progressing; she included anything she thought would amuse or interest or edify the sisters. She tells them of the people who helped or impeded her projects, of the adventures and misadventures she and the nuns who traveled with her encountered. Interviews with the great, including Philip II, or with such eccentrics as the volatile Princess of Eboli, the kindness of some, the stuffiness or obduracy of others—all receive witty and sparkling comment.

In the scorching Andalusian summers the Carmelites sweltered in the jolting, covered-in mule cart; that vehicle's flapping canvas made a poor shelter in winter when they crossed and recrossed the snow-swept plains of Castile. "Past quaking fen and precipice," through rivers in spate, they journeyed; apart from the discomfort of the mule cart there were the endless delays: axletrees broke and the nuns stood by patiently until they were mended, halts had to be made for *fiesta* processions or while the bulls were being driven in for local bullfights. Lodgings posed a problem, especially for Teresa, who was naturally fastidious; in the inns, often far from clean, the muleteers joined in the merrymaking or fighting of revelers and layabouts, heedless of the nuns trying to recite office in the alcove curtained off for them. I love her story of their arrival in the university city of Salamanca. Students were summarily ejected from a room put at the disposal of the foundress; looking at their books and belongings strewn everywhere and anyhow, Teresa observed, "Students are not very neat persons." It was the vigil of All Souls, and the melancholy trolling of the cathedral bell continued all night. Whenever a board creaked, the other Carmelite, a timid creature, imagined the worst; surely that was the step of a student tiptoeing back for his notes, his guitar, or his gown. Finally she could bear it no longer. "Mother," she quavered, "if I were to die tonight and you found yourself alone here what would you do?" To which "Mother" drowsily replied, "When that happens, Sister, I will consider the problem. Now let us have some sleep."

Saint Teresa's letters concern mundane as well as spiritual matters and vividly reflect their writer's personality.* They are addressed to all kinds of people: nuns, priests, prelates, her relatives, the king, grandees, and their ladies—persons to whom she wrote for help or whom she thanked for favors. Some are business letters, some contain instructions for prioresses given charge of new foundations. She sends cookery recipes, prescribes for ailments physical and mental, gives spiritual counsel. She scolds her sister and is affable toward her brother-in-law when their marriage is not going so well. She is courteous and diplomatic, but firm with churchmen whom she suspects of interfering with her plans for reform.

Her organizing genius, her strength of character, her powers of persuasion, her greatness of heart—all the qualities she inherited from that excellent Toledan of Jewish birth, her grandfather—are in evidence in the letters. Gaiety and humor lighten the lines. To a prioress she writes, "I am still laughing over the Sub-Prioress' accounts; imagine counting the cost of the water!" To her confessor, "Oh, Father, how you made us laugh with your account of the meals in that hospital; those dreadful cod patties." In a letter to her brother she writes, "I had a good laugh about the Master of Cere-

* The late Professor Peer's two-volume *Letters of Saint Teresa of Jesus*, which contains 437 letters, is the best English translation; the notes and Introduction are interesting and illuminating.

monies," the Master of Ceremonies being their name for the ultraproper housekeeper of a very staid Spanish gentleman. Writing to a young prioress just installed in Seville, she expresses pleasure at the news that the Jesuits are being appointed confessors to the nuns; she adds, "But these Fathers expect to be obeyed. . . . Think out questions to ask them; the Fathers of the Company like to be asked questions." The same prioress sent her some gifts and received this note in acknowledgment: "Don't send me another thing, the cost of sending them is more than their value. Thanks for the honey and the orange-flower water. Some of the quinces but not all arrived in good condition. The dog-fish was nice but the tunny-fish was left at Malagón and long may it stay there."

Hundreds of these letters are still preserved, but as many more were lost. John of the Cross kept those written to him for several years, then destroyed the lot as an act of mortification and detachment. Most of Teresa's letters were written during her last fifteen years, at stopping places on her journeys and often at midnight or in the small hours. It was during this period that her work of reform was carried out, and that despite wretched health and the increasing weight of years. At her death she left seventeen new Carmels besides reformed convents and houses of the friars. If her order knew her as a reforming foundress, the world at large came to know her as a writer on prayer and the spiritual life. Her three classics, the *Life, The Way of Perfection,* and *The Interior Castle,* were written under obedience and intended mainly for her nuns; in time these works appeared in twenty-two languages and have run to well over a thousand editions. Teresa's contribution to spiritual literature is all the more amazing when one recalls her rudimentary education—she had less than two years of formal schooling—and her early reading consisted mainly of the silly, romantic tales then in vogue.

The saint's influence on her contemporaries was considerable, as she had a natural flair for winning people to her point of view. Her father, at first opposed to her entering religion, was soon reconciled to the idea. The nuns in the little convents she founded seemed to catch the holiness, the longing for God, that emanated from their foundress; they and the friars who joined her reform exerted an influence out of all proportion to their numbers.

That influence extended far beyond the cloisters of Carmel at a period when reaction to Spain's former achievements had set in. By 1550 Spanish ambition had been sated. Teresa's grandparents had seen the end of the centuries-old Moorish occupation of the country; her father had seen and her brothers taken part in the exploration, discovery, and exploitation of the New World. Spaniards had conquered Mexico and colonized Florida; they were the first Europeans to climb the Andes, the first to sight the waters of the Pacific. But the *élan* had spent itself; the gold of the Americas had not brought benefits, much less happiness; the heady years of conquest had been succeeded by inertia, disillusionment, a general *malaise* of the spirit.

Then Teresa came, with her reminders of the brevity of life, the endlessness of eternity, the reality of God. Her watchwords, "All things pass" and "All, without God, is nothing," struck a responsive chord, recalling the true purpose of life. Her prayer, teaching, and spiritual experiences were shared with many, who in turn shared with others, a sharing that was to continue through her writings to the present day.

Since her death, many have acclaimed her. Francis de Sales heard in her message "the faithful echo of the purest spiritual tradition." Bossuet called her "the incomparable Teresa," Crashaw the "undaunted daughter of desires. . . . Fair sister of the Seraphim." Alphonsus Liguori and Henri Bergson acknowledged their indebtedness to her, while Charles de Foucauld, writing from the desert to a friend, said that apart from the Gospels her works were his only reading, "she is an author of whom one makes one's daily bread." Thérèse of Lisieux wished to be "like our holy mother, Teresa, a daughter of the Church."

She has a special significance for our own times. Seven years ago, Pope Paul VI declared her a Doctor of the Church, a title implying that her knowledge of God and the life of prayer is not only in accord with revealed truth but can benefit both believers and unbelievers in their journey to the hereafter. Earlier this century, Edith Stein, a German philosopher and university professor of Jewish parentage, came upon a copy of Teresa's autobiography, read it through at one sitting, and was so convinced that she immediately placed herself under instruction to become a Catholic and forsook her university chair for a Carmelite cell. Arrested during World War II because of her Jewish blood, she died in Auschwitz concentration camp in 1942.

As one might expect, it was Teresa's wisdom that first impressed Dr. John Wu, a philosopher steeped in the ancient wisdom of China, a devoted disciple of Confucius. He came from Buddhism, via Protestantism, to the Catholic Church. Internationally renowned as a thinker and scholar, as an authority on Christian mysticism and Chinese philosophy, Dr. Wu, apart from his work as professor in American universities, devoted fifteen years to the writing of that remarkable book *The Interior Carmel*. In it he stresses that the interior life can be lived "in the world," that we are called to imitate the saints in the spirit rather than in the letter, and that "one begins at the spot where one finds oneself."

Perhaps the most surprising tribute to Saint Teresa came from one who had been a member of the French Communist Party for thirty-six years, holding important positions in its Central Committee and Political Bureau: Roger Garaudy. At the Marxist Congress in Salzburg in 1965 he declared, "For us Marxists Saint Teresa and Saint John of the Cross are high examples of human love." Teresa must have laughed to herself in heaven, for the incident had a sequel.

In February 1970 Garaudy, philosopher, art historian, and leftist intellectual, arrived at the nineteenth Congress of the Party in Paris. The usual enthusiastic applause that greeted his call to the platform was, on this occasion, missing.

"There was a silence like that of the grave." He spoke, outlining the course he thought socialism should take in France in the changed conditions of 1970. An even greater silence followed his final words, and when the session ended the two thousand comrades turned their faces toward the walls and left an empty passage for his exit. All, even men he had formerly helped, pointedly ignored him: "Old friends avoided me as though I were a leper."

Smarting with humiliation and the sense of rejection, and unwilling to face his family while distressed, he wandered aimlessly around Paris. "Finally, without knowing what impelled me, I found myself at the apartment of my first wife, whom I married in 1937, when she had been thinking of entering Carmel, and whom I left in 1945." She had heard the news on the radio and, though they had not met for twenty-five years, she felt sure that he would come and prepared a simple meal with his favorite bread and wine. They ate in silence, then parted in silence. The last sentence of Garaudy's second book, *Parole d'homme*, reads, "I am a Christian." That was written in 1975, ten years after his tribute to Teresa in Salzburg at the Marxist Congress.

One result of our technological progress has been the pollution not merely of the world we inhabit but of the very air we breathe. This causes widespread concern and rightly so. Scant attention is paid, however, to the universal atheism that insidiously pervades and pollutes modern society, vitiating man's spiritual being and endangering his eternal destiny. Today, even more than in Teresa's day, we need reminders that God exists, that God cares; we need to be reassured that the ultimate, the only good is God, everlasting, living, and true. On that high watershed of human history, the sixteenth century, Teresa of Ávila stands, a faithful witness, testifying that there *is* a God, that she met him where we, too, can meet him—in prayer.

Shortly before her death, she wrote some lines on a marker in her office book. They read like a message to us who live in times as troubled and turbulent as her own. In those few words she comforts the anxious and reveals the secret springs of joy and peace:

> Let nothing disturb you,
> Nothing cause you fear;
> All things pass
> God is unchanging.
> Patience obtains all:
> Whoever has God
> Needs nothing else,
> God alone suffices.

# John of the Cross

## (1542–91)

### THOMAS P. McDONNELL

Juan de Yepes was born in Fontiveros, Spain, on June 24, the
son of a silk weaver in Toledo. As a youth Juan was appren-
ticed to a weaver, but when he found this not to his liking
he took a position at the hospital in Medina del Campo,
where he worked for seven years, studying during this time at
the university at Salamanca. He became a Carmelite in 1563,
was ordained in 1567, and had decided to join the Carthu-
sians when he met Teresa of Ávila, who persuaded him to
remain a Carmelite and join her in her efforts to reform the
order. In 1568, with two other Carmelites, he founded the
first Carmelite reform monastery, at Duruelo, the beginning of
the Discalced Carmelites, and took the name John of the
Cross. At Teresa's request, he served as spiritual director of
her Convent of the Incarnation, at Ávila, from 1572 to 1577.
When he refused the order of the provincial of Seville to return to Medina, he was imprisoned in Toledo. He spent nine
months in prison and was subjected to great pressure to
repudiate the reform. He steadfastly refused and finally managed to escape. While he was in prison, he experienced visions and wrote the great spiritual classic Dark Night of the

Soul *and part of his* Spiritual Canticle. *In 1579, he and Teresa and their fellow reformers were finally successful in their reform efforts, and the Discalced Carmelites were formally recognized as a separate province. After serving as head of the college at Baeza, he was prior at Granada in 1581–84 and probably finished* Living Flame of Love *and* Ascent of Mount Carmel *while there. He became provincial at Andalusia in 1585 and, three years later, prior at Segovia, and established several new monasteries in the next few years. The last year of his life was saddened when, in 1591, the Madrid chapter general deprived him of all his offices and sent him as a simple monk to La Peñuela because of his support of the moderate faction in the Discalced Carmelites in the bitter struggle that was rending the new order; he was even threatened with expulsion from the new order he had so tenaciously fought to establish. He died in Úbeda, Spain, on December 14 and is now recognized as one of the great mystics of all times and the author of some of the greatest spiritual classics ever written. He was canonized in 1726, and two centuries later, in 1926, was proclaimed a Doctor of the Church.*

John of the Cross was a Doctor of the Church who, though certainly bright enough, wasn't as ponderously bright as some of the other great Doctors of the Church. I take it with a sense of bemusement that he must have felt somewhat uncomfortable in spirit when his name was placed among the company of the scholars and intellectuals, 335 years after his death, with the likes of Thomas Aquinas, Augustine, Gregory the Great, Jerome, and all the others. And yet John of the Cross, born Juan de Yepes at Fontiveros, in old Castile, on June 24, 1542, had that special quality of mind and heart and soul that makes all the saints seem larger than life to us. But in physical stature he rose to hardly five feet above ground level. Perhaps the chief contradiction about this only fairly bright Doctor of the Church, larger than life but smaller than most men and many women, is that John of the Cross was a contemplative who was also an activist when the occasion demanded extreme measures. Even in this, however, he was an activist against his own best will and preferences. As between these ancient modalities of our both human and spiritual natures, he by far preferred peace and quiet and contemplation. Given a choice, he resisted the busybodies and the mischief-makers of this world, especially when their causes seemed just and their aspirations noble, and yet he ended up at the heart of a reform movement.

It is to his credit that John of the Cross was, in the vulgar sense, the least ambitious of saints. This in itself is a peculiar achievement for someone numbered among the Doctors of the Church, but I love John of the Cross all the more for a sweetness of temperament that saw no need to set the world on fire. (The soul, however, was something else.) I mean only to suggest that John of the Cross was not the kind of person who would become the patron saint of anything or of anyone, neither of plumbing nor of lawyers, neither of gardening nor of taxi drivers, for he was a man and saint beyond all categories of trade and occupation. If I had to name him saint of anything, I should like to think of John of the Cross as—Dante or no Dante—saint of all poets. I shall come to that later; but in a world which we all of us daily fail to conquer, lacking the talents of the great doers and makers, nothing so assuages all sense of loss and inadequacy in me as the *nada* of John of the Cross.

There is a sense of solitude in John of the Cross that seems to me more rare and more beautiful, surely, than anything I have found in Henry Thoreau of Walden Pond, who lived only a few miles from where I live now, or that I have sought in those eternal silences of Pascal or in the fierce luminosities and lonely knowledge of such people as Edith Stein and Raïssa Maritain, or that I had somehow come to share in the all but restless solitudes of Thomas Merton. I do not mean to say, of course, that John of the Cross enjoyed even the adjunct to holy solitude that Merton found so necessary in his hermitage at the Abbey of Gethsemani, in Kentucky, for it is another of the exquisite ironies of John of the Cross that he found his own greatest solitude in prison. The solitude he found there, however, was not to be tolerated as a condition that demanded his indefinite imprisonment. Therefore, as a realist, or saint with sense, he escaped.

Here's how the whole episode of the escape came about, and we ought to deal with it here, because this is no doubt one of the most significant experiences in the life of John of the Cross. To begin with, that most incisively beautiful person, the Carmelite foundress Teresa of Ávila, had come to Medina del Campo to pursue her reformation of the order and to found two reformed houses of men there. It is perhaps curiously amusing that her doing all this, in the Spain of 1568, was not regarded as anything to make women's liberation all the rage throughout the Iberian Peninsula and beyond the Pyrenees. Teresa had heard good reports about Brother John of the Carmelite friars of Medina, lately ordained to the priesthood itself, and so she was clearly out to recruit the fresh talent. Teresa was the kind of person who didn't hesitate to tell God to stop pushing, and so it was no big trick to get Juan de Yepes to go to work for the greater and reformed glory of the new Carmelites in an obscure house established at Duruelo. On Advent Sunday, 1568, the Carmelite "half a monk," as Teresa called him, renewed his profession and took the new name, John of the Cross.

I don't think we ought to bother with all that Calced and Discalced business between the established and reform groups of the Carmelite Order. I'll not pretend to be any authority on the subject. Besides, it's a rather tedious argument. In fact, when I was younger, I once presumed that Calced and Discalced referred to a peculiar dental problem among the Carmelites. Instead, it turned out to be a question of foot problems. It was, of course, much more than a question of whether the Carmelites should go about the world either shod or unshod, but of free elections going against the wishes of the authorities. Simplified or not, that's what the clash among the Carmelites was all about; and John of the Cross became Teresa's spiritual accomplice as well as her political coconspirator in the reform movement. They made steady gains among the unreformed nuns at the Convent of the Incarnation, at Ávila, where Teresa had summoned John of the Cross from his teaching duties in the Carmelite college at Alcalá and forced an election to determine a new prioress. Teresa had in fact been the prioress at Incarnation a few years before and was almost certain to be re-elected. The political heat increased to the point where the provincial of the Carmelite Order arrived on the scene to threaten supporters of Teresa with excommunication.

You can read about this frightful incident in the remarkable letters of Teresa of Ávila. In any case, Carmelites for reform won the election; but the provincial and his gang burned the ballots and set up his own candidate in office. Worse, on December 2 or 3, 1577, the provincial's boys broke into John of the Cross's living quarters and carried him off, with two other friars, to a prison cell in the Carmelite priory at Toledo. Part of this building can be seen in the famous painting of Toledo (in storm) by El Greco. The threatening aspect of that marvelous painting all too clearly indicates something of the awesome reality that surrounded John's confinement.

Gerald Brenan, in his excellent study of John of the Cross,* provides us with a detailed description of the Carmelite's desperate situation. Here is the passage from this book describing the prison cell of John of the Cross:

> This was a closet six feet by ten which served as a privy to the adjoining guest chamber. It was lit by a loop-hole three fingers wide and set high in the wall so that to read the offices he had to stand on a bench and hold up his book to the light, and even then he could only make out the print at midday. Through this opening he would hear the Tagus running in its deep trench immediately

* *St. John of the Cross: His Life and Poetry*, by Gerald Brenan, with a translation of the poetry by Lynda Nicholson. Cambridge University Press, 1973.

below. His bed was a board laid on the floor and covered with two old rugs so that, as the temperature of Toledo sinks to below freezing point in winter and a damp chill struck through the stone walls, he suffered greatly from the cold. Later, when the summer came round, he suffered equally in his stifling closet from the heat. Since he was given no change of clothes during the nine months that he was in prison, he was devoured by lice. His food consisted of scraps of bread and a few sardines —sometimes only half a sardine. These gave him dysentery, so that, like Abelard, he wondered whether the monks were not trying to poison him. As a change from this there were the fast days—at first on three days in the week, later only on Fridays. On these occasions he was taken out to the refectory where the friars sat at table, and, kneeling in the centre of the room, given his dry bread and water like a dog.

John of the Cross was also compelled to suffer the "circular discipline" treatment, or being struck on his bared shoulders with a cane or stick. Each of the friars would take his turn at it while the *Miserere* was dutifully recited. "This was the penalty laid down in the constitutions for the contumacious," Brenan writes, "and it was the severest as well as the most degrading punishment that could be given to a friar. Juan bore these scourgings in silence. The young friars pitied him, exclaiming, 'Say what they like, he is a saint,' but the older ones grew more angry than ever at his submissiveness, calling him a sly boots and a snake in the grass. He bore the marks of these scourgings to the end of his life."

The punishment and imprisonment of John of the Cross have thus been described at some length in order to give the reader at least the slightest notion of what he went through for love of Christ and fealty to cause. But even in such an age as ours, an age that stands self-accused for its violation of human rights and the cruelty of its punishments, neither cruelty nor punishment is the point when it comes to John of the Cross. Something extraordinary happened to John of the Cross during his imprisonment. Great prisoners of history

—in our own day, for example, Alexander Solzhenitsyn may be the chief exemplar—have produced an extraordinary body of literature, but it is a literature that almost always relates directly to the subjective experience of the imprisoned. John of the Cross, on the other hand, produced at least the major portion of one poem, *The Spiritual Canticle*, that arose like an incandescent dove above the dark towers of Toledo. It is an incredibly beautiful poem, one of the greatest in world literature, which defies even the tremendous commentaries written for it by John of the Cross.

The three central poems of John of the Cross—*Dark Night of the Soul*, *Spiritual Canticle*, and *Living Flame of Love*—must have been written in a glorious burst of creativity both during and shortly after his escape from the Toledo incarceration. A new and perhaps inexperienced jailer had given him pen and paper, and scholars now generally agree that John of the Cross probably composed most of the *Spiritual Canticle* in confinement and completed another, called *The Fountain*, and most likely *Dark Night* as well. The exquisite theme of escape through mystical union with the lover (God) in the poem *Dark Night* found its outward form in the Carmelite's resolve, by midsummer of 1578, to break out of jail. In all the melodrama of a James Cagney prison movie, John of the Cross had surreptitiously loosened the hinges of his cell door, a little at a time over a series of nights, while the guards slept. And then, about two of an August morning, the monk slipped by the sleeping friars, inched his way from a balcony to the city wall, and lowered himself by means of a rope he had made from strips of blankets and pieces of his own clothing. One way or another, though John would later credit the Virgin Mary with inspiring and sustaining the whole scene, he scaled yet another wall, around the courtyard, and at last found himself a bedazzled free man in the silent streets of Toledo. It said that on the first days of his escape, having found refuge in a convent of the Discalced Carmelites, John of the Cross was still so caught in the throes of poetic creativity that he dictated portions of the poems he had already conceived while in his cell but could not put down on paper.

From this point onward, John of the Cross came into his own as poet and saint and mystical theologian. Curiously, though, I am not all that impressed by the ascetical-mystical theologian and Doctor of the Church, and I should not be surprised if we have made too much of him in this regard. John of the Cross's vast commentaries on the poems—his anti-poems, the critic and translator Willis Barnstone calls them—were a studied gloss upon the poems written mainly for the edification of the Carmelite nuns. It would take a fool to discount this astonishing body of work, but to me it is all quite wonderfully beside the point. The point is the poetry itself, and apparently only a few poets in the Church have known this too much neglected fact—poets especially, I think, such as John Frederick Nims, Thomas Merton, and Roy Campbell. They know their John of the Cross more than the theologians do, though I sometimes had my doubts even about Merton. We know nothing about John of the Cross unless we ourselves have fallen in love with that Andalusian landscape of the mind that is the inscape of his poems. It was the ground of his being and the vision of his poetry, the *eros* and the *agape*, both contradiction and reconciliation.

I have connected John of the Cross to contemporary life through his incandescent poetry more than his formalized mystical theology. I insist the poetry in primary, because it is closer to the act of contemplation and the inner reality of the man himself. In our own time, surely, we can understand the contemplative who is also an activist and reformer. In an age hysterically oversexed, however, it is not so clear we can fully appreciate that John of the Cross was thoroughly sexual without resorting to genitalia. The most sensitive paradox in John of the Cross is that he was always immersed in the needs of community and yet, of all the saints, he probably had what Barnstone calls the "deepest, most withdrawn sense of solitude." There was no night so dark to him that he could not find the pristine light of day at its center. He was a man who suffered extreme punishment and cruelty but held no rancor for either his secular or his holy oppressors.

All these qualities and characteristics, I think, have meaning for us today—to say nothing of the fact that I sense John of the Cross to be a saint in whose presence we would not have experienced either social discomfort or spiritual embarrassment. Greatness of spirit makes an easy companion. I felt this way in the presence of Thomas Merton, in his Gethsemani hermitage and surrounding woods and fields, when I was lucky enough to have worked with him on a collection of his writings later published as *A Thomas Merton Reader*. I mention this not for the sake of name-dropping, since I really don't know many such names to begin with, but simply as an indication of the way a beautiful spirit can inhabit a given space in the world.

I have the final notion that John of the Cross is the saint who may now stand with us at the edge of the space age. Perhaps the most astonishing thing he ever did, in my view, was the little pen-and-ink drawing left in the care of the nuns at the convent of the Incarnation, at Ávila. This sketch is known as the "Christ Crucified" drawing and is said to have derived from a vision experienced by John of the Cross. What is so conceptually and graphically stunning about the John of the Cross crucifixion is that it is perceived from a point in space. I don't think that in the whole history of perceiving the Christian crucifixion anyone had thought—or, more likely, had dared—to look at the most tremendous fact of our human drama in quite this way. As René Huyghe says in a note on the drawing, quoted in the Kavanaugh-Rodriguez edition of the *Collected Works of St. John of the Cross*: "The vertical perspective—bold, almost violent, emphasized by light and shade—in which he caught his Christ on the cross cannot be matched in contemporary art; in the context of that art it is hardly imaginable."

Some four hundred years after John of the Cross, the Spanish painter Salvador Dali developed the visionary sketch of the poet into one of the greatest paintings in contemporary art and, surely, the most remarkable one in the entire history of crucifixion art. The Sunday supplements and the artist himself have contrived to make Dali into a slightly mad public figure, the surrealist creator of limp watches and the like, but there is not the slightest doubt that he must be ranked as one of the greatest painters and draftsmen of the century. His "Crucifixion of St. John of the Cross" and other religious paintings are recognized masterpieces in an age given almost entirely to a type of modernism that identifies with its time, to be sure, but that almost just as certainly is not timeless. I'll not attempt here anything like a verbal description of Dali's extrapolation of the John of the Cross drawing. It has to be seen, if only in the best possible color reproduction, and it has to be contemplated. Just to look at this painting, however, is to contemplate it to some degree or another. There are infinite depths in the Dali re-creation of the John of the Cross crucifixion, which you never see in quite the same way twice, and one of these impressions came out in a poem I wrote some years ago, published in *Spirit* magazine and slightly revised as follows:

## CRUCIFIXION
*On Viewing Dali's Christ of St. John of the Cross*

Sail yourself from earth a farewell while,
A wry observer, X, spun in space,
Whose mind rejects the convenient grace
Of purely graphic worlds;
Project dark distances in vertigo of light
That leaps across the listless years,
Let go the bloodbeat heart and fleshfall fear—
Stand ready to depart:

Is that the worldcross
Where eternity cracked in the quake of time?
Mountains and oceans sway,
Fine dimensions break—
All history is racked in pain, our pinpoint deaths
Intersect Good Friday's rage of ruin—
Look down, exile, love gestates your birth,
You can't escape the dialogue of earth.

A man oughtn't to be compelled to say more than his fairest contemplative effort allows, so I shall have to let it go at that. If I had to say more—and to sum up in those words my feeling for, and understanding of, John of the Cross—it would have to be from a letter of Teresa to Mother Ana de Jesús, prioress of the Carmelite nuns at Beas, who, at one point, didn't think too much of Father John of the Cross as a confessor and spiritual director, or what the current fashion would call a guru. Anyway, here in part is what Teresa said in reply: "I am really surprised, daughter, at your complaining so unreasonably, when you have Padre Fray John of the Cross with you, who is a divine, heavenly man. I can tell you, daughter, that since he went away I have found no one like him in all Castile, nor anyone who inspires people with so much fervor on the way to heaven. You would not believe how lonely his absence makes me feel. You should reflect that you have a great treasure in that holy man, and all those in the convent should see him and open their souls to him, when they will see what great good they get and will find themselves to have made great progress in spirituality and perfection, for our Lord has given him a special grace for this. . . . I can assure you I should very much like to have Fray John of the Cross here, for he is indeed the father of my soul."†

† *The Collected Works of St. John of the Cross,* translated by Kieran Kavanaugh, OCD, and Otilio Rodriguez, OCD. Institute of Carmelite Studies. Washington, D.C., 1973.

# Francis de Sales

## (1567–1622)

## JOHN DEEDY

*Born in the family castle in Thorens, Savoy, on August 21,
he attended the Jesuit college of Clermont, in Paris, from
about 1580 to 1588 and then studied law and theology at
Padua the next four years, receiving his doctorate in law
when only twenty-four. Despite prospects of a brilliant secular career and despite the opposition of his family, he decided
on a religious life and was ordained in 1593, when he was
also appointed provost of Geneva. He spent the next five
years in the Chablais, where the efforts of the Duke of Savoy
to impose Catholicism on the people of this area of his do-
main by military force were being fiercely resisted. Despite
repeated attacks on him by assassins and crowds of Calvinists,
he was most successful and attracted thousands back to Catholicism. He was made coadjutor to the bishop of Geneva in
1599 and succeeded to the see on the death of the bishop, in
1602.*

*He became one of the outstanding leaders of the Counter-
Reformation, noted as a confessor and preacher and for his
intellect and wisdom. He wrote several spiritual works, among
them* Introduction to the Devout Life *(1609) and* Treatise

on the Love of God (1616), *both of which stress that sanctity is possible in everyday life and are still widely read. In 1604 he met Jane Frances de Chantal, became her spiritual adviser, and with her, in 1610, founded the Order of the Visitation (Visatandines). He died in Lyons, France, on December 28. His beatification the year he died was the first formal beatification to be held in St. Peter's. He was canonized in 1625, declared a Doctor of the Church in 1877, and designated patron saint of journalists in 1923. His feast day is celebrated on January 24.*

I presume the saints are still up there working for those less militant of the Church Militant. I say "presume" because I haven't been troubling them as much in recent years as I used to in the days of what Michael Novak called "gimme"— that time when we asked God through the saints for everything from good weather to lost umbrellas. Like most other middle-aged Catholics, I can remember when, in time of trouble, stress, anxiety, hope, a virtual flood of ejaculations would run through my mind en route to the saints. Francis de Sales had a prominent place in that recitative—first, because I had a first-class relic of him (still do, for that matter) and it seemed an unwonted waste of a precious resource not to be calling on a person, a piece of whose hipbone or elbow was in a reliquary on the dresser in the bedroom; secondly, Francis de Sales had a special place in my prayer life because I felt a kinship with him by reason of a wonderful annual outing enjoyed for years with marvelous people, all in his name. This came each February in conjunction with the Catholic Press Month Mass held in Boston; Francis de Sales is, of course, the patron of the Catholic press.

The Mass was sponsored by *The Pilot*, of Boston, and was celebrated in one or another chapel in downtown Boston. We staffers at the *Catholic Free Press*, the counterpart diocesan publication in Worcester, forty snowy miles to the west, would drive down the old Boston-Worcester Turnpike for the liturgy, presided over, as a matter of course, by Archbishop Richard J. Cushing. After Mass was done, *Free Pressers* would repair to a fine restaurant, toast Francis de Sales, then banquet and drink to one another's health—not necessarily in that order and, in the course of the evening, not necessarily remembering Francis de Sales. I remember, for instance, a particularly pleasant "observance" at the Red Coach Grill in Framingham, where—under the influence of Julie Harris and her tippling Sally Bowles in Isherwood's *I Am a Camera* spin-off—we did ourselves in inordinately with champagne cocktails.

I don't know whether they hold that Catholic Press Month Mass any more. I do know, looking back from a distance of almost twenty years, that those were unholy/holy/wonderful times. They might have been a dubious expenditure of subscribers' money (except we were modestly paid —and how!—and for three dollars a year subscribers were getting more than their money's worth). In any case, I really don't think Francis de Sales would have disapproved of those outings, were he consulted. Sure, he was "big" on austerity, as today's vocabulary would have it. But good times linked to holy occasions are never to be despised. Besides, it was hard enough getting through winters in Worcester; we needed the pick-up Francis de Sales made possible each February. The Catholic Press Month Mass in Boston, accordingly, was therapy as well as spiritual pilgrimage, from which we returned sated and refreshed—if more by camaraderie than by grace. Francis de Sales would not have begrudged this circumstance.

I miss those outings as I miss the colleagues that made my stint in official Catholic journalism such a pleasant part of life and career, though not one I would wish to return to; in Thomas Wolfe's overworked phrase, you can't go home again.

More to the point of this essay, I miss Francis de Sales and chide myself for letting him become so peripheral to my life. Today it is only in some kind of personal emergency that I tend to remember Francis de Sales—as when I threw my back out recently while straightening a throw-rug (alas the travail of middle age). Before reaching for the Sloan's Liniment, I reached for the relic—proving I guess, that the days of "gimme" aren't quite so dead, at least for some of us. But, bad back or other emergency, Francis de Sales merits remembrance not just for *auld lang syne* or therapeutic possibilities but for his relevance—a relevance supported by personal and ecclesiastic authenticity.

Authenticity? Certainly! With the discoveries of recent years that many of our "saints" have been fabrications, heroes and heroines of mistaken identity or imagined existence, or developments of pious traditions, it is reassuring to know that someone as admirable as Francis de Sales cannot possibly be a Philomena. His place in history is completely documented and solidified by a body of work amounting to twenty-six volumes: sermons, essays, letters, meditations, books, including that priceless volume *Introduction to the Devout Life*. The old *Catholic Encyclopedia* of the Gilmary Society described *Introduction to the Devout Life* as a work intended to lead "Philothea"—the soul living in the world—"into the paths of devotion, that is to say, of true and solid piety." The *New Catholic Encyclopedia* speaks more clearly. It cites the book as a classic that "sets forth a spirituality compatible with life in the world," a book that therefore, "stands in contrast to the works of those contemporary authors who regarded perfection as attainable only by withdrawal from the world." That evaluation is now dawning on those of us who once had this book on the bedside reading table.

*Introduction to the Devout Life* contributed as literature in no small way, they say, to the development of the modern French language: it was that crisp and precise and beautiful. To those of us who read and meditated on it, the book provided a glimpse, however fleeting, of saintly perfection. It also provided a glimpse—through its clarity, its warmth, its charm, its economy of words in delineating large ideas—into a person and stylist who merits remembering and emulating, whether canonized saint or not.

That person looms larger by the centuries—the more for those looking for instruction in his life, since his career could have been a family-induced disaster. There's a theory—tenuous, to be sure—that privilege is a debilitant and that one has to be forged in the schools of want, or desperation, or persecution, the better to become a person of heroic virtue. Francis de Sales's life debunks all that. His could have been a priesthood of privilege. The Savoyard aristocratic strain of blood on the mother's side, the father's proud position in the secular society—these gave the family inordinate influence in the councils of Church and state, and, in fact, resulted in Francis' going straight from the altar of ordination to the high post of provost of the Church of St. Peter in Geneva. A worldly family disappointed in the eldest son's choice of vocation could take consolation; at least the son would not be an inconspicuous cleric.

Beginnings such as that have had their counterparts a thousand times over. And admittedly, family favor is not the most inspiring of starts, however innocent the recipient of benefaction be of the solicitation, as Francis de Sales appears to have been. But Francis de Sales's life dramatizes that privilege and well-placed family do not inhibit the development of character—not always, and not necessarily in the larger number of cases. It comes down again to the individual; we are what we make ourselves. And Francis de Sales became what he made himself. Take an example: Francis' father was livid when he learned that his son intended to leave his sinecure and take on the dangerous work of re-evangelizing regions of the Chablais, on the south shore of the Lake of Geneva. He rushed to the chancery in an effort to bring an end to "this piece of folly." He didn't succeed—and Francis would not change his mind. Francis went off, as the enterprising and independent young person always must—indeed, as the young Jesus did when he preached in the Temple and as numerous others of less divine station have since. Family ties can be allowed to be only so strong, and the best-intentioned of parents must be thwarted when they threaten to stifle that which they love. But that's an old lesson, isn't it?

I don't know whether Francis de Sales's father was still around when his son became bishop of Geneva. The honor would have pleased him—and reconciled him undoubtedly to his son's career. And, of course, the father would have taken pride in the son's fame as a preacher. Francis de Sales was the superstar of the Lenten sermon-series circuit, when these were the Catholic Church's Chautauquas. He was in demand in the most prestigious cities and dioceses, and it was while giving the Lenten sermons at Dijon in 1604 that he met Jane Frances de Chantal. We know the happy result of that coming together: the founding of the Visitation Order of nuns, devoted to the care of children and the poor. Of course, too, the father would have taken pride in the son's astonishing, unselfish industry. Francis de Sales catechized, counseled (*Introduction to the Devout Life* actually grew out of notes of instruction and advice written to a cousin who had placed herself under his guidance), administered his diocese, and wrote, wrote, wrote to the end of his days. His days were relatively short; he died at fifty-six.

The further point of all this, of Francis de Sales himself, is that he was a remarkably open and available man, a man who gave of himself and was constantly reaching out to hearts and minds. In that sense, as well as in his gifts of expression, he becomes the perfect model for anyone associated with communications as they relate to the faith. His depth was profound, but his mode was easy and conversational. Thus, when he went to Rome, sometime around 1600, to be examined by Pope Clement VIII, Baronius, Bellarmine, Frederick Borromeo, and other exalted personalities on his fitness to become coadjutor of Geneva, Francis de Sales astonished all with the simplicity and accuracy with which he could manage the knottiest of subjects. It was the same talent that even now is the key to his writing. On his feet, he had an orderly mind; so, too, in his writing, along with the added patience, lost to so many of today's writers, of being willing to rewrite and rewrite, rearrange and rearrange, then add new material, which in turn would necessitate more reconstruction. His tremendous gift through all these steps was never to lose the touch that made him understood to those of more modest learning, nor less erudite to the learned.

I often wonder whether much of organized religion's problem today rests in the inability of its communicators, at typewriters as well as in pulpits, to convey the meanings of faith in terms that at the one time can reach both the lettered and the unlettered. The insultingly simple and confusedly abstruse have been the bane of religion through long stretches of its history, their thoughts and books sometimes not gathering the dust they deserved. Far too rare has been that person of reason and insight who is capable of taking the cosmic concepts of faith and conveying them in words so readily graspable and convincing as to touch lives and influence actions. In my experience as an American Catholic and writer, I have known only two who were unmistakably gifted in this regard, and one ended up going whacky on a narrow theological point, while the other drifted to another Christian denomination, undercutting among some his work of many decades. Most, like myself, have been journeymen of a sort—although I suppose there is something to be said for journeymen; some can be quite effective, and indeed several have been in modern American Catholicism.

But back to Francis de Sales and two qualities in the man without mention of which no paper on him would be complete.

The first is a detail that is not so frivolous as at first might seem the case: his love of books. Of course Francis de Sales came from a family that could afford books when they were as yet a luxury item, and eventually he lived a life to which books were central. But as books have been swept from the hand reach of so many in our day by films, by television, by leisure-time preoccupations, so could they have been swept from Francis de Sales's interest by comparable divertisements of his day, such as the riding, dancing, and fencing that he took up as a youth and pursued as a young man in order to satisfy the whims of his status-conscious father. Francis de Sales did not let these activities sway his mind from the fact that books are basic to the serious man, a lesson in his life that loses nothing of its strong point over the centuries. One of the most appalling things, to me, about former President Gerald Ford was that he did not read books, and no revelation about his life went further in explaining his limitations. And I've heard educators complain that the most dismaying thing about many of their students is the lack of impulse to pick up a book other than ones that they are required to for their courses. This is not the making of a society distinguished by its wisdom.

Finally, that second great quality in Francis de Sales: his humility. He lived, as I mentioned earlier, a life of austerity, a life that was a sign to the people by its very simplicity. He sought no honors, no special privileges. The loftiest of associations did not turn his head, so to speak. In 1622, the Duke of Savoy, en route to meet Louis XIII at Avignon, invited Francis de Sales to come along. Anxious to obtain from Louis certain concessions for the French section of his diocese, Francis, by now quite unwell, went. Two things were remarkable about that trip: Francis de Sales insisted on living his usual austere life while at the royal court; secondly, he made himself available to the crowds that flocked to see him (his fame was that genuine) and to the religious houses that pleaded with him to come to preach to their communities. The exertions took their toll. On his way home Francis de Sales stopped at Lyons at the convent of the Visitation. He was dying, yet he still would accept nothing grand. He insisted on occupying a small, poorly furnished room in the gardener's cottage, and there he died, the victim of a cerebral hemorrhage. A short time before death came, he was asked by a nun to write down what virtue he especially wished the sisters to cultivate—he being unable to converse at this point. On a piece of paper, Francis de Sales wrote one word in large letters: "Humility."

Today's journalists are not expected to pursue their careers in the fashion of humble monks, but if Francis de Sales's life urges on them any one last point, it is humility in what they put on paper. This lesson from Francis de Sales's life is more subtle than others might be. He did not carp on the point. He let it become self-evident throughout his twenty-six volumes in the calm and reasonableness and understanding of his presentations. These qualities are the essences of humility in the professional journalist; their opposite is arrogance, a constant temptation among traffickers in words. At the risk of ending on a note of preachment, St. Francis de Sales stands as an example of the effectiveness of the former and the unnecessariness of the latter. From the point of view of a professional journalist, it is probably the most important lesson of his life for any moment of history.

# Vincent de Paul

## (c. 1580–1660)

## JULIE KERNAN

*The son of French peasants, Jean Depaul and Bertrande de Moras, and the third of six children, Vincent was born in Pouy, France, on April 24. He studied at the college at Dax and the University of Toulouse and was ordained in 1600. While returning from Marseilles in 1605, where he had gone to recover a legacy left him, he was captured by pirates and sold as a slave in Algeria. He eventually secured his freedom, went to Rome for further studies, and then became chaplain to Queen Margaret of Valois in Paris. In the following years his work with the poor and his sermons attracted attention. His meeting of Francis de Sales in 1618 led to his appointment as ecclesiastical superior of the Visitation, and the following year he became chaplain of galley slaves waiting to be shipped abroad. He founded the Congregation of the Mission (known as the Vincentians or Lazarists) in 1625, devoted to missionary work among the peasants. The congregation soon spread to all parts of France. He also began to establish parish confraternities to aid the poor and, with Louise de Marillac, in 1623 founded the Sisters of Charity. He established hospitals and orphanages, ransomed Christian slaves in North Africa, helped better priests' formation by founding new seminaries, and wrote widely on spiritual subjects. The friend of royalty and the nobility, his whole life was devoted to the alleviation of human suffering and misery. He died in Paris on September 27. Canonized in 1736, he was declared patron of all charitable groups by Pope Leo XIII in 1885.*

Charity—the very word brings before me the figure of a thin, sturdy man in the clerical garb of the seventeenth century, a broad-jawed face somewhat lengthened by a short beard, the big nose of a Gascon, lined features, and a neck sunk into his shoulders. The brown eyes under heavy brows are keen and penetrating, and a quizzical smile adds to the vivacity of his expression. Vincent de Paul did not live so many centuries ago that we lack authentic portraits of him, although they were painted in his later years and, we are told, under difficulties; in this case great reluctance was shown on the part of the sitter. He had laid it down that a man should not consider himself or his person.

Yet when he died, in his eightieth year, "Monsieur Vincent," as he was called by his contemporaries, was known far beyond the borders of his native country. The confraternities and institutes he had established for the relief of spiritual and human distress had spread through Europe, into Africa, and into the future. In the age of turmoil and religious bigotry or indifference following the fratricidal wars of religion in France, he had awakened consciences to a sense of brotherhood and community not only among the affluent and highly placed but among the poor themselves. The counselor of royalty and nobility, he had enlisted the help of these in his charitable undertakings.

Those who describe Vincent de Paul mainly as a humanitarian or philanthropist oversimplify the wellspring of his activities. He loved God first, and that love overflowed to his fellow humans and practical deeds in their behalf. He did indeed love men and understood them better than most. He respected the dignity of the most destitute and deprived, and his charity toward them was marked by meticulous consideration of the needs and feelings of each. What he taught was the practice of eyeball-to-eyeball charity in the name of Christ.

Vincent would have been the last to consider himself a "founder" or originator of new ideas. His genius lay in his ability to co-ordinate and transform into action the ideas and charitable impulses of others; his secret, to lay everything in the hands of Providence. He started many of his enterprises because circumstances obliged him to do so. As opportunities arose, his fertile mind conceived of new and flexible forms to *personalize* the charity he considered as the duty of every man and woman.

From the beginning, he had involved the laity in his works. The first confraternity he established in the ravaged countryside at Châtillon, in Dombes, was of peasant women. To these women he gave a role more complete and independent than ever before. In cities, his Ladies of Charity were recruited from court circles and other women of influence; from varying backgrounds, they function today in parishes of the Catholic world. Confraternities of laymen aided him in his lifetime and in succeeding generations formed associations working under his inspiration. Two hundred years after Vincent died, Frédéric Ozanam banded together the men of the Society of Saint Vincent de Paul, who still bear his principles in mind and apply his methods.

To the two religious institutes Vincent brought into being, he gave new forms. Previously, works of mercy had been carried on chiefly by members of religious orders and pious foundations. His Congregation of the Mission (also known as Vincentians or Lazarists) was initiated as an association of secular priests, devoted to the spiritual care of dechristianized rural areas, living and working among poor people. The Sisters of Charity, established by Vincent with the co-operation of the widowed Louise de Marillac, attended the sick poor, "their convent the sickroom, their chapel the parish church, their cloister the streets of the city." Soon they were working in hospitals, homes for foundlings and orphans, insane asylums and prisons, even in armies, where some of them served as the first women nurses. And because at that time no public education was provided, they became teachers of both religion and secular subjects.

It somehow brings me closer to Vincent to realize that he was not naturally the serious, solid man who radiated goodness and humility, whose serenity and equilibrium attracted and persuaded those who crossed his path. In one of the few glimpses he gave of himself, he told that he was "of a crabbed disposition and prone to anger." His escape from the dour life on his father's farm, where he tended the pigs, sheep, and cattle, and his efforts to acquire an education, he attributed to ambition and self-seeking. He also told that because the Church offered opportunities of a kind no other profession opened to a poor peasant boy, he became a priest to secure a comfortable living from the stipends and benefices of convents and abbeys dispensed in that day by France's rulers.

Hard knocks, it seems, were needed for Vincent's evolution. Was he not shipwrecked by pirates and sold on the slave block in Tunis? Was he not unjustly accused of theft? Did he not endure injuries at the hands of those he had befriended? From such experiences he had drawn a lesson and even profited. "The works of God," he was to say later, "achieve themselves, and those that are not His soon perish."

After years of study, travel, and adventure he came to Paris, around the age of twenty-seven; at least ten more years were to pass before he clearly saw the road that he must follow. Restless and impulsive, he had begun to suffer from uncertainties and scruples, when he placed himself under the direction of Pierre de Bérulle, the first great reformer of the French clergy, who guided his steps for a number of years thereafter.

These things I learned later. It was in Paris, where he was

to spend the greatest part of his life, that I first "met" Monsieur Vincent. As I had grown up in the Catholic parish of a large American city, I had heard frequent mention of the Ladies of Charity and the Saint Vincent de Paul Society; I had seen Vincent's sisters working in orphanages and hospitals, but I had no curiosity concerning their origins. I had to live in Paris to learn something of the man who inspired them. My first interest stemmed from a chance encounter, and one step led to another as my predilection for the saint increased. For three years between two world wars, I lived in the quarter around the rue du Bac, where Vincent's memory is most alive today. On that street is the mother house of the Sisters of Charity and, on the rue de Sèvres, close by, the headquarters of the Congregation of the Mission. I rarely went out without seeing the cassocked priests hurrying by or the white cornets and bright blue garb of the Sisters of Charity. (Since Vatican II, I have found them clad in conservative dark dress and head veils—a pictorial loss but one, I think, the practical Monsieur Vincent would have approved.)

Because I was asked in a letter from a friend at home to call on the two American assistants of the superior-general of the world organization of the Sisters of Charity, I went one Sunday afternoon to the address that I was given. It did not take long, after the warm, even affectionate, welcome I received from Sister Madeline Morris and Sister Mary Reeves, to be drawn into their orbit. As I met the other sisters, I realized my two new friends were representative of the diversity of good deeds carried on by each.

I had no such personal contacts with Saint Vincent's sons. I was, however, kindly received when I asked to see their chapel, where are enshrined the remains of Saint Vincent himself. In a separate room I was shown some of his poor possessions: a cassock, its buttons snipped off; a large cloak in better condition; three heavy shoes; a hair girdle; a breviary; a small wooden crucifix with bronze figure; a candlestick; bed curtains of a coarse material.

Moving as were these poor relics, I preferred to think of

Vincent de Paul in life. Around that time I was given the three-volume edition of his life and letters by Père Coste, with its fascinating illustrations of personages associated with the saint, also maps and scenes of seventeenth-century Paris. There was not a quarter of the present great city over which he had not moved, first on horseback, then walking with a cane when, still comparatively young, he was afflicted by a disease of the legs from which he never recovered. I sometimes tried to picture that limping figure as I walked through the city piled up with so much history.

I also found traces of Vincent's passage in the section of Paris known as Clichy. As pastor of what was then an immense parish of farmers, fishermen, and laborers extending from the present center of the city to the northern walls, he discovered the joys and servitude of the parish priest. The little church he rebuilt is still standing, in it the pulpit from which Vincent preached. In the garden is a very old tree said to have been planted by Vincent, and an old baptismal font, on it the date 1612.

So great was Vincent's zeal and love of his people that he wished to reside at Clichy indefinitely, but Bérulle considered his proven abilities as worthy of a wider role. At his inducement—some say command—Vincent became tutor, then spiritual adviser and counselor of the pious and charitable household of Count de Gondi, general of the royal fleet.

It was with the aid of the Gondis, who promoted and funded his Congregation of the Mission, that Vincent could eventually live in his own way. He first took his little band to the college of the Bons Enfants, and after 1612 to the Priory of Saint-Lazare. Originally a leprosarium (hence the name) and practically deserted, it was offered to Vincent and his companions with its immense ramshackle building and the fields around it, an area long since given over to office buildings, shops, and two great railroad stations and their yards. For twenty-eight years Vincent made Saint-Lazare his headquarters, working from early morning until late into the night. From these humble surroundings he directed his network of organizations, conducted a vast correspondence (three thousand of his letters are said to have been extant at the time of his death), held retreats for those preparing for the priesthood and many of the most famous of the ordained clergy, went to court when necessary as a succession of rulers of France requested his advice on religious matters under authority of the throne, and directed and implemented throughout France what we might call today "social welfare."

His great charity is apparent in the letters he wrote on spiritual and practical matters dealing not with his own concerns but with the needs and problems of each correspondent. His ways of praising, encouraging, even admonishing indicated his warm heart and courtesy; they were also at times amusing. To his sisters who in time of war engaged in nursing, he wrote: "Young women to have the courage to go to the battlefield . . . to visit the poor wounded not only in France but as far away as Poland! Ah, my daughters, is there anything equal to this?"

"A queen has no need of jewels," he was heard to observe gently to Anne of Austria as with a trace of human regret she handed over to charity some of her valuable ornaments. To one of his priests he admonished: "Don't you think, Monsieur, that if you had been a little less intent on doing things your own way, you might have been just a little more careful!"

Vincent's fairness and tolerance is shown in all that he said and did. "Bitterness has never served any other purpose than to embitter," he said. In an age of partisanship and religious bigotry, following the Huguenot wars, he instructed his priests to approach the members of other faiths "gently and humbly, so that it may be seen that what is said proceeds from a compassionate, charitable, and not a bitter heart."

He was not an innovator in liturgical or theological matters. He loved the services of the Church as prescribed in his day and insisted on their careful observance. Still it is not likely that he would have resisted any changes that might bring God closer to the heart of the worshiper. He also wrote: "Cannot the Church, which never changes in the things of faith, not do so with respect to discipline? And has not God, who is Immovable in himself, not changed his ways in dealing with men?"

Most orthodox in his beliefs, he yet refused to testify at the trial of the Abbé de Saint-Cyran, fiery leader of the Jansenists, who had been his friend. Nevertheless, Vincent was the person most responsible for the condemnation of the heresy by Rome. He said that he had done the first to save a man, the second to preserve the faithful from the errors that man had spread.

"The Church of our own day would not be as we know it, if the little shepherd of the Landes had not lived, thought, and acted," wrote Daniel-Rops, French historian and one of Vincent's biographers. With Cardinal Bérulle, Vincent played a leading role in the reform of the clergy, a vast enterprise undertaken, with great difficulty and delay, according to the principles laid down by the Council of Trent. Even more important was Vincent's part in the foundation of seminaries for the training of priests, a command of the Council of Trent left somewhat vague as to practical application. Vincent was the first in France to open a "major" seminary. To this cause he diverted the efforts of his Congregation of the Mission. In Italy, in Germany, in Spain, in Portugal, in Poland, Vincent's procedures for clerical training were followed.

The forms of religious life initiated by Saint Vincent, as we know, were new. In the case of the Sisters of Charity especially, their status was not that of religious in the sense of nuns or sisterhoods before their time. Their institute was called a "company," their residence a "house." They were not required to take vows; when, after four years, Louise de Marillac persuaded Vincent to allow her and her companions to do so, it was with the understanding that they were "private and for one year." This company was the first of what in modern times have proliferated as "secular institutes."

It was, however, in his concept of charity that Vincent de

Paul made his most notable contribution to the Church. He gave new meaning to the role of the parish as the center of the spiritual life and charitable and communal activity of its members. With changes brought about by economic and social conditions in modern times, Vincent's principles and spirit have also been applied to projects for relief work and human development on a national basis and between the countries of the world. Caritas, an international organization, functions in seventy-three nations to bring assistance to disaster-stricken and war-torn areas and to the poverty-ridden of the Third World.

After the industrial revolution, when wealth was accumulated by a few while many others lived in poverty, it became evident that charity alone could not accomplish what was needed unless associated with the idea of "social justice." The coexistence of social justice and social charity has been stressed by the popes down to today.

Despite the appearance of social theories that deny or question the merit of charity, the works and spirit of Saint Vincent continue and flourish. In *Quadragesimo anno*, Pope Pius IX said: "Even if someone should obtain all that is his due, a wide field will remain open for charity. Justice alone, even though faithfully observed, can remove the cause of social strife but can never bring about a union of minds and hearts. Only when this is obtained will it be possible to unite all in harmonious striving for the common good, when all victims of society have the intimate conviction that they are members of a single family and children of the same heavenly Father."

To this, Vincent de Paul would have been the first to say amen.

# Anne-Marie Javouhey

## (1779–1851)

### GLENN KITTLER

*The daughter of a well-to-do farmer, Balthazar Javouhey, and Claudine Parisot, Anne was born in Jallenges, France, on November 10, and early decided to devote herself to the poor and the education of children. She joined several groups of nuns in her youth but was unable to find her proper niche with them. However, it was while with one of these groups in Besançon that she had a vision of black children that was to influence the rest of her life. In 1807, on the advice of Cistercian Dom Augustine Lestrange, she, her three sisters, and five other women were clothed with the habit (she took the name Anne-Marie) by the bishop of Autun. Dedicated to the instruction of children, their congregation quickly expanded all over France, but it was their purchase of a former Franciscan friary at Cluny in 1812 that marked the beginning of the Congregation of St. Joseph of Cluny. The educational methods she used in a school she opened in Paris in 1815 attracted widespread attention, and in 1817, at the request of the governor, she sent her first group of nuns to open a missionary school for blacks on Réunion, a French island east of Madagascar. Its success led her to extend her activities to*

*Africa and French Guiana. She spent the years 1828–32 su-*
*pervising the colonization of Mana, in Guiana, at the request*
*of the French Government. In 1834, the government as-*
*signed her the task of educating six hundred slaves, who were*
*about to be set free, on how to cope with freedom, an enter-*
*prise that evoked world-wide interest. After leaving Guiana, in*
*1843, she spent the rest of her life establishing new*
*houses of her congregation in Tahiti and Madagascar. She*
*died in Paris on July 15 and was beatified in 1950.*

There are thousands of saints on the calendar of the Church.
They came from various centuries, various countries, various
walks of life, various ways of life. And yet they all had one
thing in common. Because of the lives they wanted to live,
they all developed a unique sensitivity to the Will of God.
Once they were spiritually confident that they knew what
God wanted them to do, nothing could detour them. This
cost many of them their lives.

Another trait many saints had in common was that they
knew what they wanted to do with their lives at a very early
age. Such was the case with Anne-Marie Javouhey, who was
teaching catechism to other children and to adults before she
herself was ten years old. Even earlier, she had told her father
that she wanted to become a nun. He patted her gently on
the head and told her to go and play with her dolls.

Ever since I first learned about Anne-Marie, twenty years
ago, I have been profoundly impressed and inspired by her
steadfastness. Not once did the flame of her vocation flicker,
which was amazing in view of the many storms it faced. As I
got to know her better and was able to read some of her letters, I reached the point where I could read without raising a
brow at her frequent statement: "I know this is what God
wants me to do."

Nanette—which is what she was called by those closest to
her—couldn't have announced her vocation at a worse time.
Born in France in 1779, she was only ten when the French

Revolution erupted. In the minds of the revolutionaries, the Catholic Church was in the same class of enemies as the Bourbon rulers. Church property was confiscated; monasteries and convents were closed, the priests and nuns fleeing to other countries.

Priests who wanted to remain in France had to take a pledge of allegiance to the new government which superseded their vow of obedience to the Pope. Many did, and because they did they were stripped of their sacerdotal faculties by Rome. Also, bishops were no longer appointed by the Pope but were elected by local political councils. Rome refused to accept these bishops, but it didn't matter. Outwardly at least, the Church was dead in France.

Inwardly, however, the Church in France was very much alive, and Nanette was a lively part of it. She continued her catechism classes, sometimes in the family garden, sometimes in the barn, sometimes out in the woods; and when lookouts warned her that government agents were approaching, she quickly switched from catechism to mathematics and spelling or geography, returning to catechism when the agents departed.

And this. Roving through the Catholic underground in France were a number of loyal priests in disguise, risking their lives to bring the sacraments to the faithful. Only here and there were there Catholics who could still be trusted. Nanette was one of them. Now and then, a stranger would arrive at the Javouhey home and through hints and clues, would let Nanette know who he was and that he knew who she was.

Then Nanette would plead with her father to let the priest hide in the attic for a few days, until she could make contact with the local faithful. Always her father resisted, terrified of what would happen to his family if the priest were caught in the house, but always Nanette won out. Then, a few days later, on the pretext of attending a party at the Javouhey home or a picnic in the nearby woods, the faithful would arrive, and there would be confessions and Mass and Holy

Communion. Next, it was up to Nanette to arrange safe passage for the priest to his next destination.

Perhaps it is the drama of Nanette's life that appeals to me. I have always loved a good adventure story, and Nanette's life was full of them. She was often in combat with bishops, with colonial governors, with her own government, even with members of the congregation she started: the Sisters of St. Joseph of Cluny. She went into the rugged mission fields of Africa and South America, and once her ship almost sank in a storm at sea. More than once, she was close to death from tropical diseases. This is more than enough adventure for any one person, but it becomes of spiritual value only when it has spiritual motivation, and Nanette had a bottomless reservoir of that.

Nanette had a great devotion to the Blessed Sacrament. During the revolutionary years, when she could not receive Communion often, she would prepare herself for a secret Mass by spending the day before in silence, prayer, and fasting and then spend the day after in the same way, in thanksgiving.

One day she demonstrated how real her love for the sacrament was. It was in the early days of her congregation, and she and a few other nuns were running a crowded orphanage in Souvans. Nanette ran out of money, and she could think of only one place to turn for help. She went to a nearby church, proceeded down the main aisle to the Communion rail, opened the gate, and crossed the sanctuary, and then she went up the steps to the altar and knocked on the tabernacle door.

"I need help," she said aloud. "I know that I have been imprudent, and perhaps I have gone beyond your will in many ways. But I have done it for the children. They are more yours than they are mine. If I have made mistakes, punish me—not them. I beg you, don't forsake them. Please, please help."

She lowered her head, astonished by her audacity. The voice she heard was clear and firm. It said: "Why have you come here to expose your doubts? Have you no faith in me? Have I ever disappointed you? Go back to the children."

Nanette returned to the orphanage fully prepared for a miracle. Without hesitating, she went to the pantry and swung open the door. The shelves were as empty as they had been when she left for the church. Wincing, she shut her eyes. "Forgive me for being presumptuous," she whispered, "but I had hoped—"

She heard the wheels of a cart upon the cobblestones in the courtyard. She went to the door and opened it. She saw her father approaching in a cart overloaded with food. He was still opposed to the life she had chosen, and his expression now was full of self-disgust. He called to her: "I don't know why I am doing this, but I suppose I can't let you starve."

Nanette knew exactly why he had done it: Her Beloved Lord in the tabernacle had put the decision into the man's mind hours before she had knocked on the door.

Earlier, Nanette's father had been so opposed to her vocation that she moved out of the house to an uncle's home. It was there one morning, kneeling in front of a priest who was holding up a consecrated Host, that she took the temporary vows of a nun. Later, relenting, her father let her enter a convent in Switzerland. One night, she awakened from a deep sleep and found her room brilliantly illuminated. Within the sphere of light stood a woman in a nun's garb, and she was surrounded by children who had black skin, brown skin, bronze skin. Nanette had never seen such children before in her life.

The woman said, "These are the children God has given you. He wishes you to form a new congregation to take care of them. I am Teresa. I will be your protectress."

Many years passed before the vision became a fact, and when it did the world entered a new era.

It came about like this: First, Nanette did form her own congregation. After several years of struggle and slow growth, the congregation had enough members to send some to the missions. Nanette sent the first group to Senegal, in West Africa. Later she visited the Senegal mission herself and for the first time saw in the flesh the black children she had seen in her vision. She also saw their parents, and she was shocked by how cruelly Africans were being treated by the European colonials. She vowed she would do something about it. At one point she accompanied a group of settlers to French Guiana, in South America, to establish a new community, and she observed how African slaves in the country were being treated even worse. She became even more determined to do something about it.

Around 1830, a strong anti-slavery movement developed in France, and Nanette, back from South America, was part of it. The newly installed government of King Louis Philippe indicated that slavery would soon be abolished throughout the French Empire. This brought roars of objections from slave-owning colonials around the world. The colonials insisted that Africans simply did not have the intelligence to take care of themselves outside of Africa and would only cause a lot of trouble if they were set free. To appease the colonials, the government declared that if the freed Africans did not prove their competence in seven years they would be returned to slavery.

In French Guiana, five hundred freed slaves walked off their owners' farms and went into the capital town of Cayenne. They could not find jobs, they ran out of money, and they eventually became a serious public burden. There were threats of violence. The colonials pleaded with Paris to rescind the abolition edict.

King Louis Philippe knew about Nanette's earlier work in French Guiana with the French settlers. He summoned her. He asked if she thought it was true that Africans could never learn to take care of themselves outside Africa. She called it nonsense. Then he asked if she would be willing to return to French Guiana, take those five hundred ex-slaves out of Cayenne, and help them establish their own community elsewhere in the country. She said yes. She knew just the place—a plateau on the Mana River, a place called Mana, just in from the sea. She had been there herself.

For two days, Nanette conferred with the king, telling him all she knew about French Guiana. When the time came for her to leave for her ship, the king accompanied her to her carriage to say good-by. As he watched her depart, he said to those near him: "Take my word for it, my friends. Madame Javouhey is a great man."

She proved it. Understandably, perhaps, the colonials wanted Nanette to fail. Not only did they refuse to support her, as the king had instructed, but they confiscated her supplies, they arrested any of her people who went into Cayenne on business, and they actually organized a plot to assassinate her. When she refused to take orders from the bishop of French Guiana, he placed an interdict upon her, banning her from the Holy Communion that was the core of her spiritual and physical strength.

She fought on. Five years later, when the inspectors came from Paris to appraise her work, they were amazed at her success. The town was neat and clean, the people happy. There were a school, a church, a clinic, an orphanage. Small farming and small industries were thriving. Mana was better off than Cayenne itself. And that was the beginning of the end of slavery throughout the world.

Nanette returned to Paris a celebrity, but she still had her enemies. One of them was the bishop of the diocese where her headquarters were located. For years, the man had been trying to take control of the congregation; for years, Nanette had resisted him. And he was still trying.

One day in March 1851, Nanette, then seventy-two years old, was walking along a corridor to her office, when she suffered a stroke and went into a coma. Doctors were sure she would not recover. For weeks, her condition wavered. On June 8, she sank dangerously low, and people thought this was the end. In the morning, however, she was slightly improved. During the night, news arrived that the bishop had died, and it was decided to keep the news from Nanette until she was stronger. She was told a week later, on June 14.

She took the news calmly. "So he has died, that good bishop," she said. "God rest his soul." She remembered her own condition that night of June 8, and she smiled. "We almost met, he and I, on that very day, before the judgment seat of God. So he's gone in ahead of me, that good bishop. Well, that is correct; that is how it should be. A bishop should always enter first."

When Nanette founded her congregation, she adopted as its motto "The Holy Will of God." On July 14, 1851, still ill, she said unexpectedly to those in her room: "I have been thinking about our lives together these past forty-five years and I am amazed by God's generosity to us. We have been very blessed. It is a great reward for obedience—all that we have been permitted to do. Always follow the Holy Will of God."

She died the next morning, after, she disclosed, spending the night praying for the bishop.

Nanette—Blessed Anne-Marie Javouhey, if you prefer—has become my favorite saint. Her love for people and her desire to serve them was surpassed only by her love for God and her desire to serve Him. God's love for her can be evidenced by her victories in this life and in the next. Many miracles have been attributed to her, as she continues to love and serve us. I can't claim Nanette has performed any miracles for me, but perhaps my devotion to her has protected me from any need for miracles. There is much in Nanette to emulate: her love of the Church, her love of the sacraments, her love of the poor, her love of the downtrodden, her humility, her obedience to the Will of God. A little more of all of that in each of us could change the world almost as much as she did.

# Anthony Claret

## (1807–70)

### ROBERT E. BURNS

*The son of a weaver, he was born on December 23 in Sallent, Spain, and as a youth pursued his father's trade. He entered the seminary at Vich in 1829 and was ordained in 1835. After a time in a Jesuit seminary in Rome, ill health caused him to return to Spain. During the next decade he gave retreats and missions throughout Catalonia. In 1849, he was mainly responsible for the founding of the Congregation of the Missionary Sons of the Immaculate Heart of Mary (the Claretians). He was appointed archbishop of Santiago de Cuba in 1850 and labored to reform the see and improve the condition of the people there against bitter opposition, including an attempt on his life in 1856, when he was seriously wounded. The following year, he returned to Spain and became Queen Isabella II's confessor, though his main interest was in the missionary activities of his congregation. He resigned his see in 1858 and was appointed director of the Escorial, where he encouraged interest in literature, the arts, and science. He was active in efforts to revive Catholicism in Spain and preached some ten thousand sermons and published some two hundred books and pamphlets during his lifetime. He accompanied the queen into exile in France when the revolution, in 1868, drove her from the throne. After attending Vatican Council I in Rome, in 1869–70, he retired to a Cistercian monastery near Narbonne, France, and died there on October 24. He was canonized in 1950.*

Anthony Mary Claret is the kind of saint who has suffered especially at the hands of the traditional hagiographers. He was not a martyr, although he suffered greatly the impositions of both friends and enemies. He wrote prodigiously, but he was not a scholar like Thomas Aquinas or an author whose wisdom, like Augustine's, would echo down the corridors of time. Although a man of affairs of two continents, the dramatic confrontations of a Thomas More were not to be his. Not even the easily conceptualized "little way" of a Thérèse or a John Vianney could be ascribed to him.

So, what could his biographers say of him? Predictably, they said that he was pious, chaste, industrious, unselfish, and humble (some were not too sure about the latter virtue), all good Boy Scout, or less charitably, bourgeois virtues. In thus viewing him superficially, they, in the words of an American folk song, "done him wrong."

Claret's reputation has also suffered from the handicaps of his being the founder of a religious order. (This identification has not depressed the reputations of Francis, Dominic, Ignatius, or Benedict, but, then, there are those legions of their followers.) This can be a handicap in several ways. There is no doubt that founders of religious orders are disproportionately represented on the roll of canonized saints. Countless mute, inglorious saints undoubtedly go unrecognized because there is no fellow order member to act as fulltime postulator of the saint's cause and because there is no one to raise the funds to promote and pursue the tortuous cause to formal canonization.

The reputation of a religious-order founder can also suffer in a second way. Loyal and loving daughters or sons of the founder often take pen (or Selectric) in hand to sing the praises of the holy founder. Overwhelmingly edified in advance of this labor, they feel it unnecessary to seek out the truly distinctive and extraordinary attributes of the holy person. Too often they spin a pastry web that may be confectionary but is rarely nourishing. The beloved subject of their well-meaning labors is thereby placed at the top and unenviably required to rise above it.

I first heard of Anthony Mary Claret nearly thirty years ago, and I confess that for a number of years I was turned off by his friends and biographers. The incidents that seemed to abound in accounts of him struck me as cloying, and when I dipped into his *Autobiography* (in what may have been a poor translation), the saint struck me as smug and even a little priggish. That I did not give up on him is fortuitous. My close association during all these years with men who follow him as Claretian fathers and brothers forced me to look beneath surface impressions, to discover a truly extraordinary saint.

In the first layer beneath the surface of Claret's life (and believe me, there are other layers), a student of the saint's life will find that he appears to be a man of contradictions. Indeed, Pope Pius XII, in his 1950 *Discourse to Pilgrims for the Canonization*, took note of this:

"A great soul, seemingly born to bring about the marriage of opposites. Humble in his origins, yet glorious in the eyes of the world; small in body, yet a giant of the spirit; modest in appearance, yet quite capable of commanding the respect of even the great ones of this earth; strong of character, yet possessed of that gentleness learned through the restraint of austerity and penance; always in the presence of God, even in the midst of his prodigious external activity; slandered, yet admired; celebrated, yet persecuted. And in the midst of all these marvels, a sweet light illumines everything: his devotion to the Mother of God."

Allowing for a certain rhetorical fullness to be expected in such discourses, this description of the saint is strikingly factual. There was indeed in Claret's life, as in the lives of many saints, a continual dialogue, often a continual struggle between opposing tendencies. But his efforts to reconcile these opposites had many unique characteristics.

Of one thing we can be certain. Claret's apostolic labors were of heroic proportions. Reading the accounts of his personal activities (and remember that these are well-documented records of a saint of the past century), we are reminded of St. Paul's own accounts of his prodigious apostolate.

As a young priest in Spain, he begged permission from his bishop to be a roving missionary in addition to his parish duties. Apparently a speaker of exceptional magnetism, although he spoke little Castilian and only the Catalan dialect of his native area, Claret attracted huge crowds, including many who came from great distances. "Once they heard him," we are told, "they waited outside his confessional for hours, even for days, with lunches they brought from home." Another account of a mission, in the town of Olot, is typical. "Although he himself heard confessions as long as fifteen hours a day ('I was never much for sleep,' the saint wrote), twenty-four other confessors were kept busy also. And three priests spent the entire morning distributing Holy Communion."

When, in 1848, Claret was sent to the Canary Islands to avoid entanglement in a civil war in Catalonia, he plunged into missionary work there with characteristic fervor. The pastor in the town of Telde, there, wrote to his bishop:

"This town has never seen the like of it. The most bitter enemies have made peace. Scandals, both public and private, have been terminated, and amends made. Broken marriages have mended. Restitutions have been made. Why? Because no one can withstand the fire of his preaching, the kindness and liveliness of his manner, his forceful reproofs . . . and the impact of his reasoning. The appeal of his words breaks his listeners' hearts, and everybody, even the proudest nature, falls at his feet weeping."

But the prodigy of Claret's work reached its ultimate when he was sent to Cuba to become archbishop of Santiago, a diocese that embraced one half of the Cuban island. One terse summary of his four-year episcopate there is enough to indicate the staggering breadth of his apostolate:

"Reforms the clergy, creates new parishes, sends a missionary team to preach continually throughout his diocese. He himself makes three pastoral visits to the whole diocese, traveling on muleback and on foot. With Mother Antonia Paris, founds the Congregation of Teaching Sisters of Mary Immaculate. He sets up credit unions and establishes the Confraternity of Christian Doctrine. He continues writing and distributing books and pamphlets."

Claret's constitutional inability to procrastinate almost led to his death and probably led to his recall from Cuba. The most volatile subject in that country then was the race question. Slavery was an important fact of economic life, a necessity dear to the hearts of the rich and powerful. Although interracial marriage was expressly forbidden, interracial concubinage was common. Without hesitation, Archbishop Claret rejected this injustice and legalized more than ten thousand marriages. On one of his pastoral visits, a fanatic embittered by this action attempted to kill Claret and seriously wounded him. While he was returning to Santiago from this trip, the ranches of two families who had hosted him were burned.

The chronicle of Claret's apostolic work would require many more pages than we have here, but it should be noted that in a lifetime so engaged he strove continuously in what might seem to be the opposite direction, in the direction of a deeper spiritual life.

In his early twenties, after he had worked for four years in a Barcelona textile mill, Claret felt himself drawn strongly to the contemplative life. He wished then to become a Carthusian, and he made serious efforts to fulfill that wish. He gave up this desire reluctantly in obedience to his spiritual director, and although he later realized that the contemplative life was not for him, he struggled almost until his death to deepen his spiritual life, to provide sanctifying soil in which to root his apostolate.

If one seeks a single unifying constant in the seemingly contradictory events of this multifaceted man, one might find it in Claret's realism. Realism and, beyond that, practicality. The distinguished writer Paul Claudel, who spent years in Spain as the French ambassador, once noted that in Spain, unlike most other European countries, there had never been a truly romantic movement or era. Realism, he believed, was too deeply ingrained in the Spanish soul. And this is easy to see in the life of Anthony Mary Claret.

There is, in the first place, the simple, straightforward style of his *Autobiography*. When I first read this unpretentious work, in my ignorance of the saint's great complexity and subtlety of character and the extraordinary depth of his sanctity I misconstrued its simplicity. When I read, "I was barely six when my parents sent me to school. My first schoolmaster . . . never punished or upbraided me but I was careful not to give him any cause for doing so. I was always punctual, always attended classes, and always prepared my lessons carefully," an image of Goody Two-shoes leaped to mind. Or again, speaking of his grandfather, Claret wrote: "It was at night and his eyesight was failing and I guided him through the obstacles with such patience and kindness that the poor old man was very glad to see that I hadn't run off to join my brothers and cousins who had abandoned the two of us."

But the extraordinary explanation for what seems to be a holier-than-thou attitude is a rare and holy ingenuousness. Whatever good Claret did, even as a little boy, was to his unquestioning mind a gift from God for which he neither took nor deserved credit. Quoting the Book of Wisdom, he wrote: "'I was a boy of happy disposition. I had received a good soul as my lot.' That is, I received a good nature or disposition from God, out of his sheer goodness."

I believe that Claret's pervading realism was grounded in this never-questioning trust in God. He went about doing the work that confronted him, without a thought of sparing himself or saving something for tomorrow. If God willed that he do something else, some infirmity would force him to turn away (although he was incredibly healthy) or his superiors would direct him elsewhere. That was the way God worked, and Claret wasted neither time nor energy wondering whether the change was for the best.

The intense practicality of the saint seems to have been both mystically and culturally induced, and the implications of it may, more than anything else about him, make Claret a saint for our times.

Consider, for example, the fact (and this surely is rare in the community of saints) that Claret had a gift, perhaps even a genius, for technology. Born in 1807, at the start of the century of the rise of industry, he was put to work as a boy in the "well-equipped little thread and textile factory" of his father. At the age of eighteen, despite his long-held belief that his vocation was to the priesthood, Anthony obeyed his father and went to work in a large Barcelona textile factory. "Who would have guessed," he wrote, "that God would one day use in the interests of religion the studies in design that I undertook for business reasons?"

With typical openness he noted, "God gave me such a ready wit in this that all I had to do was analyze any pattern and in short order a copy would emerge from the loom exact to the last detail, or even with improvements if my employer so desired."

But the urge toward the priesthood became so strong that he turned away from a highly promising career in manufacturing. Nevertheless this child and almost prototype of the new industrial age brought the influence of technology to bear in his priestly labors.

I have already recounted in some detail the almost incredible personal labors of Claret. But this was not enough to satisfy him, and with his appreciation of technology, he multiplied his efforts many times by establishing publishing houses in Spain, in the Canary Islands, and in Cuba. Using the most advanced technology then available, the religious publishing house he established in Spain alone had distributed four million pamphlets and books by 1866, four years before his death. Long after his death, the publishing houses he founded continued to distribute religious books in great numbers.

Claret himself, of course, was an indefatigable writer of books and other tracts. A bibliography of his published works requires eight typewritten pages.

Another example of Anthony's practicality is his approach to the social problems he found in Cuba. The situation there, one that ironically still prevails in much of Latin America, was one of extreme disparity between the wealth of a handful of landowners and the miserable poverty of the landless majority. The archbishop, believing that spiritual progress would be difficult if not impossible under these conditions, moved without delay to remedy some of the injustice he found.

In his *Autobiography*, Claret tells us:

"I bought a ranch for the poor of Puerto Príncipe. By the time I left Cuba I had spent 25,000 duros of my savings on it. . . . My object in starting this ranch was to gather together poor boys and girls, many of whom were wandering the streets begging. At the ranch they were fed, clothed, and taught their religion, as well as reading, writing, and whatever trade they wanted to learn. One hour—and only one hour—a day they had to work on the ranch. This provided enough food to make the ranch self-supporting."

Both through projects such as this one and through the credit unions he established, Anthony, who knew nothing of agriculture but taught himself the subject with typical diligence, taught as many as he could to become self-sustaining. He placed particular importance on their diversifying crops to offset the one-crop (sugar) tyranny of the large landowners, who used this means to keep the poor dependent on them.

The practicality of Claret is also evident in the religious congregation of men that he founded in 1849, the Congregation of the Missionary Sons of the Immaculate Heart of

Mary, known popularly as the Claretian fathers and brothers. Realizing that most of the religious orders existing at the time were committed to particular apostolates (teaching, contemplation, missions, hospitals) and wishing to expand his own apostolic zeal beyond Spain "to the world," he conceived of an order that would have the flexibility to go anywhere and adapt itself to prevailing needs as they arose. This had been the pattern of his own apostolate, as we have seen, meeting whatever needs confronted the Church wherever his congregation was invited. So, together with five other priests willing to accept this challenge, he began the Claretians.

Less than a year later, he was summoned and told of his appointment as archbishop of Cuba. He was thunderstruck and resisted the appointment in view of his obligation to the fledgling community. He refused the appointment several times and accepted it only after his own bishop commanded it. Even then, despite the enormous energy he expended in Cuba, he never left the little and soon-to-be-growing band he founded.

He continued as its spiritual director until his death, and he wrote the congregation's constitution. Some of the latter document reflects the time in which it was written, but much of it is as practical today as it was then. In the year before his death (1869), he wrote from Rome to Father Xifre, then superior-general of the congregation:

"I am delighted to hear that you have undertaken a foundation in Chile. . . . America is a great and fertile field, and in time more souls will enter heaven from America than from Europe. This part of the world is like an old vine that bears little fruit, whereas America is a young vine. I have been pleased with my visits and dealings with the bishops who have come from over there. . . . If it weren't for [his final poor health] I'd fly [sic!] there myself. But since I can't go myself, I visit the American College here in Rome."

In keeping with Claret's practical design for his congregation, the Claretians came by invitation to Mexico in the late-nineteenth century and to the United States in the early part of the twentieth for the specific purpose of working among the Spanish-speaking. This mission continues until the present, but the work of the Claretians in this country has evolved in a number of other directions, to meet the needs of the day.

Anthony Mary Claret was pre-eminently, then, a man of action, a person of prodigious physical accomplishments. But we haven't begun to exhaust his charisms. Not only does he continue to bear witness to Jesus and Mary through the more than four thousand members of his congregation (as well as their countless thousands of lay associates) but also we have hardly begun to mine the rich vein of his unique spirituality. It is unique, I think, because of the kind of person he was, intensely active but always seeking spiritual depth. It is unique because, although God showered mystical insights on him from childhood, his realization of these gifts had to be earned the hard way.

Claret forced himself to meditate for long hours, but the classic perfection of the meditative saints was never to be his. He found it necessary to pray vocally (rather than mentally). Yet he persisted in a dogged adherence to his plan for spiritual growth with the same precision that had been prefigured in his designs for the textile factory in his youth. And apparently with the same conspicuous success.

I suspect that students who take the trouble will find in the life of Claret new depths of understanding of the Eucharist—his gift of conserving the sacramental species incorrupt from one communion to the next boggles the mind—and of the unique role of Mary in salvation history (a deposit that has been all but bankrupted by her well-meaning but misguided friends).

It is, of course, a cliché to describe a saint as "for our times," and God forbid that we should try to pre-empt the title of that other great saint, "a man for all seasons," but there is in Anthony Mary Claret, I think, a timelessness that makes him a model appropriate for our time—among others.

# Thérèse of Lisieux

## (1873–97)

### Naomi Burton Stone

*Marie Françoise Martin was born in Alençon, France, on January 2, the youngest of nine children of Louis Martin, a watchmaker, and Zélie Guérin. Her mother died when she was five, and the family moved to Lisieux, where she was raised by her elder sisters and an aunt. Two of her sisters became Carmelite nuns, and though refused when she first applied, she was accepted by the Carmel in Lisieux a year later and professed in 1890, taking the name Thérèse of the Child Jesus. Suffering from tuberculosis, she endured her illness with great patience and fortitude, devoting herself to prayer and meditation, serving for a while as mistress of novices. At the order of her prioress, Mother Agnes (her sister Pauline), she began to write in 1894 the story of her childhood, and in 1897, after finishing this the previous year, at the order of her new prioress, Mother Marie de Gonzague, she also told of her life in the convent. Both accounts were eventually published as* The Story of a Soul, *which has become one of the most widely read spiritual autobiographies of modern times. She died in Lisieux on September 30, quickly attracted a tremendous following as the Little Flower and the "saint of the little way," and was canonized in 1925. Her feast day is celebrated on October 1.*

If I were asked to think quickly of the attributes I most admired in Thérèse of Lisieux, I would say her self-discipline and her courage. She could be so gracious to people with whom she had little natural affinity that they wondered why she found them so attractive. She accepted physical pain and bereavement with fortitude and without complaint. At a time when she was experiencing spiritual revelations of great depth, she was able to write her young cousins cheerful, "silly," and delightful letters, with no reference to her inner emotions. She had learned early in her life that talking too much about a personal, perhaps miraculous, event could somehow spoil it.

Given to vocal and facial expressions of love, hate, pleasure, or woe, I constantly struggle to keep my feelings to myself. Unsuccessfully. Thérèse took herself in hand when she was about nine years old and had only thirteen years to achieve perfection. I was better at saying the right thing when I was nine than I am today. I convinced my widowed father that I was delighted with his plan to remarry—not the woman of my choice—while all the while a black demon was growing in my heart. The Christmas I was fourteen and every girl in my class was getting a gold chain necklace, I received a watch. I covered disappointment just enough to avoid questions around the tree, but my sister was told to find out what was wrong. (To spare my father's feelings we worked out a compromise. I had longed for a watch with a second hand so that I could time myself holding my breath in boring classes —an explanation my father seemed to find perfectly reasonable. An exchange was made.) Since then, it has been downhill. On Valentine's Day my husband gave me an enormous straw hat: "to wear in the garden," "to shield you from the sun." I stared with amazement at the hat and said, "Me? A hat? I *worship* the sun" and ran upstairs to bite off the tip of my tongue. It is rather painfully obvious why, if I were looking for a model to help me improve my ways, I would fall for Thérèse. But, in some ways, not so obvious after all.

What did first draw me to her? I had never even heard of her as a child. There have been no new saints in the Anglican Church since the Reformation, and it was in that Church I grew up. I was alive when Thérèse was canonized, but I doubt it was widely reported in the London newspapers. I must first have seen her name in Thomas Merton's *The Seven Storey Mountain,* but like so much that was Roman Catholic in that book it eluded me, for the first conversation I can remember having about her was with my English godmother, whom I met in New York through, of all people, Ian Fleming. It was during the year before I became a Catholic, a time spent in tentative but frequent sorties into Catholic churches. I was fascinated by statues and vigil lights, learning gradually to distinguish between Anthony (Christ Child+loaves of bread) and Joseph (Christ Child+T square). The statues in one New York church were a real culture shock—Lucy with her eyeballs held out on a plate in front of her—and my godmother usually agreed with me.

But when I spoke disparagingly about Thérèse, the too-sweet expression, the festoons of red roses, there was a short silence. My godmother finally said: "You know, during the First World War, French generals, as well as ordinary soldiers, used to carry a copy of her life—*The Story of a Soul*—into battle. They considered her an extraordinarily brave person, not at all a pink-and-white, spun-sugar type. . . ."

The words might easily not have registered, but there was something about the tone. This was not the expected response. It stopped me in my tracks. I decided to take a look at the autobiography that had swept through the world from its first publication, in 1898, and continued to do so. I read it. I consider it one of the most marvelous graces that God has given me that I loved it, and loved its author, from that day on.

The edition I read was Michael Day's translation. There is

a note in it that ". . . diminutives and interjections, natural enough in French but rarely used in English, have been omitted." It is possible that I may have escaped some of the "sentimentality" that disturbed readers in mid-twentieth century. In the 1940s and '50s there had been an explosion of investigative journalism into Thérèse's life and writings: Had the sisters falsified her writing, which they did indeed edit? Why had they touched up photographs and so widely circulated a pretty painting from memory by her sister Céline? Was it true that Thérèse had been mentally ill as a child, her gifts mere neurosis? As I remember it, this was not done to diminish Thérèse but to make her, unadorned, unedited, appeal more to the modern reader's passion for truth at all costs.

Actually attacks on her had been going on for years. I was extremely fortunate to be given early in my study of Thérèse Father Henri Petitot's book *Saint Teresa of Lisieux*, first published in England in 1927. In his Preface he quotes from a contemporary and intemperate source: "[She] is a brazen and puerile plagiarism of St. Teresa [of Ávila] . . ." and so on to charges that the Carmel at Lisieux and the clergy had combined to "manufacture a modern saint who should be a fruitful source of revenue to the diocese of Bayeux and Lisieux." Father Petitot describes Thérèse's spirituality, showing its originality. He discusses its negative aspect, in the sense that he was against rigorous mortification, asked for no special favors such as ecstatic visions; had no fixed method of prayer, no "multifarious activity." He writes:

> The saint who is most appreciated, admired, and invoked in the twentieth century is not, as one might have expected, a nun devoted to the most charitable and active form of apostolate, but a young nun who entered Carmel at the age of fifteen, who died at the age of twenty-four, and who did nothing but pray, suffer, and obey. She did not nurse the plague-stricken, the poor, the sick, the aged; she did not save her country, as Joan of Arc did; she did not bring back the papacy from Avignon to Rome, as St. Catherine of Siena did; she did

not do any great deeds, and yet we find her exerting an unparalleled moral influence throughout the world.

Before I had even heard of most of them, Father Petitot answered for me many of the same objections to Céline's portrait and the edited manuscript that were still being made and refuted some twenty-five years later.

It would not be true to say that I was impervious to the criticism of friends who did not share my enthusiasm for the Little Flower. It was a time when I was, probably ostentatiously, gulping down large helpings of Garrigou-Lagrange, the noted theologian, on the mystic life, a time when someone hearing I was devoted to Thérèse, or Teresa, would say "The Big One, I presume?" "Er, no," I would have to say, "the little one." Raised eyebrows. I admit that she did not sound a likely choice for an intellectual snob. But I had been helped past the flowery Victorian phrases and the pretty pictures to the true metal. She was very much my kind of ideal. And we did have some things in common. I knew the warmth of family life in a comfortable, not wealthy, home; I had experienced the death of my mother at an early age; I could share her addiction at one time to floods of tears over small matters; I, too, had been in danger of being spoiled by a loving father and sisters; I, too, was stubborn, but the difference was that I had not turned that trait into great fortitude. She dealt stoically in her last years with physical suffering but, far more than that, she did so when for years she had no sensible perception of God's presence, and yet her faith never wavered. The more I read the more I saw that "little" Thérèse was a giant.

While I hope I had as much admiration for Teresa of Ávila as did her namesake, it was the little one that stole my heart and presented me with a goal that was certainly not easy of attainment but nonetheless not so impossible that it seemed useless even to set out toward it. I loved her for so many reasons: the Christmas she was told she could no longer expect her shoes to be set by the fireplace and filled with little gifts, was no longer a baby. She stormed upstairs in a fury. Took herself in hand and soon came down, tears gone, determined not to let anger get the better of her again.

I loved her for her spunk: for insisting on speaking to the Pope at an audience when she had expressly been forbidden to do so by a high-ranking prelate. And this at a time when nicely brought-up young ladies did not call attention to themselves in public. I was charmed with the picture of Thérèse and Céline racing off from their father, the guide, and the whole pilgrimage, down to the lowest level of the Colosseum, closed to visitors, where she knew the martyrs had spilled their blood for their faith.

Maybe it all sounds like rather small beer, but it seemed to me a measure of her passion for living, her impetuosity, which she learned to harness. Once in a while one meets a person who has overcome a headstrong temperament, perhaps a quick temper, and always the struggle seems to show not in a worn-out passivity but in a quiet and shining strength. There was a simple directness in Thérèse. It meant a great deal to her to stand where the martyrs stood, so she went after her objective in a straight line.

It is more than twenty years since I found Thérèse. One wonders how she would strike one today. I suspect that the language of her writing would be more easily recognized as a product of the age and circumstances of her life, would be seen as charming rather than sentimental. Once, I gave a copy of *The Story of a Soul* to a young friend who had just joined the Army. He was a brilliant writer, not a Catholic, and I was hesitant about the gift. But I soon had a letter from basic-training camp saying the book was terrific. He had found it peculiarly comforting when he had to leap from his bed in pre-dawn darkness and stagger out on parade, to remember that in all her days in Carmel Thérèse had never felt really warm, that she often could not sleep from the cold —and had never once let anyone know. "Wow," he wrote, or some such intellectual comment.

Rereading her collected letters,* I realize what an amount of firsthand material we really have. Thérèse had a passion for writing, little notes, long letters, a real need to communicate with her family. It reminds me of another silent contemplative—Thomas Merton—who from a monastery shared his thoughts with the world.† Thérèse's writing, either the letters or the three sections of her autobiography that were written because she was told to write them, are very frank. Although she had never wavered about being a nun in an enclosed order, she still had dreams of being a missionary, even wished she were a priest. Lest that be made too much of at this particular moment, I think it should be added that in the same passage she says she would like to experience all forms of martyrdom, be a Crusader, to die on the battlefield for the Church, to preach the gospel in every continent. And she says, too, that with all her desire to be a priest she admired Saint Francis and envied his humility in refusing the honor of the priesthood. I think that what we can find in her writing is a great openness, a readiness to discard old ideas not because they were old but because they did not seem to her profitable in perfecting the life she had chosen.

She was in many ways far ahead of her time. In the Carmel where she spent her last nine years the rules were strict and there were many of them. It was customary to admire saints who had practiced bodily penance as a way to holiness. She herself had an attraction to mortification soon after she entered the convent. She secretly devised ways of making her

* *Collected Letters of Saint Thérèse of Lisieux.* Edited by Abbé Combes. Translated by F. J. Sheed. Sheed & Ward, New York, 1949.

† Reading *The Seven Storey Mountain* again, I wondered whether Merton had continued to be as close to Thérèse as he was the night he prayed at her shrine on the ground of Saint Bonaventure University: "If I get into the monastery, I will be your monk. Now show me what to do." Not long ago, I was listening to a tape in the series *The Mystic Life*—talks Merton gave on Sufism in the spring of 1968. He had not forgotten her. Making the Christian connection, he said as an example, "St Thérèse—the Little Flower—a perfect Sufi!" with a smile in his voice.

food tasteless. "I gave that up a long time ago," she told one of her sisters. "When food is to my taste I bless God for it; when it is bad, then I accept [it] . . . such unsought mortification seems to me the safest and the most sanctifying." She had also at one time worn a little iron cross, but when it bit into her skin and caused an infection she discarded it and learned a lesson. "The macerations of the saints were not made for me nor for the little souls who are to walk in the same way of childhood." Father Petitot writes:

> The more she advanced in age and wisdom, the more [her] reading, observation and reflection confirmed her in mistrust of violent and blood asceticism. In her last years her conviction in the matter had become so absolute and peremptory that she thought it her duty to give her sister this parting recommendation: "One must be on one's guard against [it]. Believe me, never launch forth on that way; it is not meant for very little souls like ours."

She saw in the exaggerated penance—the hair shirt and such austerities—the danger not only of injury to physical health, which might prevent one from doing one's work properly, but the greater danger of self-complacency.

Thérèse's way of life meant that she accepted what God sent her way, the good along with the bad. As little girls she and Céline had been given a collection of dolls' clothes and scraps of material. Céline chose a brightly colored piece of cloth. Thérèse took one look and said, "I choose everything," and took charge of the whole basket. She did indeed choose everything. She suffered deeply through the three years of her father's last illness, when he had lost his mind. Though many may have thought she had advantages in having two elder sisters in the convent and later Céline and one of her cousins she loved so much, it was often more painful than joyful. She herself said that the convent was not their childhood home. Things were different and must be so observed. She never took advantage of her sisters' presence or asked for special favors.

I see even more clearly today than when I first read her autobiography that Thérèse was an innovator. Depending more and more on the Gospels for her inspiration, this young girl in a little-known convent in France figured out for herself an approach to God that would appeal to millions. It was a departure from the sum of prayers and penances, sacrifices, prostrations, that were still considered the ideal. Her way of life is very simple, and as so often happens, complete simplicity turns out to be just as difficult, if not more so, than colorful acts of self-denial. What is harder, really, than smiling and making people think you are having a great time when you are bored to distraction? How hard it is to avoid showing you are hurt when unjustly accused of doing wrong! Yet every day provides the raw material for living the Little Way, Thérèse's idea of a short cut to Heaven. As she wrote: "We live in an age of inventions now, and the wealthy no longer have to take the trouble to climb the stairs—they take a lift. That is what I must find—a lift to take me straight up to Jesus." And she searched the Scriptures and found the confirmation she sought. She could remain very small and insignificant and rely entirely on God's mercy to lift her up. All on her own she discovered that small is beautiful and that, for some of us, small is best.

I have an idea that if one is hooked on Thérèse, one stays that way. In the post-Vatican II chopping and changing of the calendar, I admit I have not always been a faithful follower—nor ever deserted her completely. In my room, near my desk, is a photo with three roses stuck in the frame—one a gorgeous, now dusty, red-silk creation by Dior, which I know bears her stamp of approval. I am convinced that her big heart and level head make her a saint to whom anyone could tell anything. Someone once said to me, "Oh, don't pray to her. All she sends is crosses." And there may be a little truth in that. Thérèse clearly considered the pain and suffering in her own life as a sign of God's special love for her. A sign (and a love) she is most willing to share with us. Her answers to prayer may not always be what one has expected or even wanted, but they always turn out to be the ones that are exactly right.

# The Unknown Saint

## FULTON OURSLER, JR.

*Obviously there is nothing to say factually about the Unknown Saint. Suffice to say that there are thousands of men and women through the centuries who, unknown and unrecognized, lived lives of holiness. Perhaps even more than the famous and well-known saints, they can provide inspiration and hope for us in the twentieth century, since their lives are much closer to those of most of us than those saints whose heroic virtues and wondrous deeds we can admire but hardly hope to emulate. With those saints specifically listed in the Calendar of Saints, the Church recognizes and honors those lesser known but equally worthy of emulation, on the feast of All Saints, November 1.*

Thirty years ago, not long after I had become a convert to Catholicism, I heard a remarkable story during a sermon at the church of Saint Francis of Assisi in New York. The tale was apocryphal, the priest explained; he did not remember where he had heard it. The source, he suspected, was anonymous.

The story concerned Anthony of the Desert, the hermit whose heroic spirituality had inspired painters, writers, and the faithful of many denominations for more than fifteen hundred years. Anthony had decided that he could not be close to God in the cities and villages of man, the tale began, and so he had journeyed into the desert and made his home in a cave, where he could pray undistracted even by meadow, river, or flower.

In the first response to Anthony's prayers, God sent to the hermit, in a series of visions, the very temptations he had fled: young women who offered sexual delight; men who flattered, who promised riches and political power. Then devils appeared in the form of ravening beasts. The temptations were explicit, unremitting, torturous. Anthony suffered almost to the moment of death but never wavered in his devotions. At length, he was released. The visions disappeared, and God told Anthony that only one temptation remained.

The hermit was to leave the desert, go to a certain village, ask for the sandalmaker, and knock on his door. Anthony could ask the man any question, said God, but could not reply to the questions that the sandalmaker might ask him.

After a long journey, Anthony found the village. It was late at night when he reached the cobbler's house. He knocked and the door was opened.

"Are you the sandalmaker?" Anthony asked.

"Yes, and who are you?"

"I cannot tell you," said Anthony.

"Why have you come here?"

"I cannot tell you."

The sandalmaker studied the man before him. He seemed exhausted; perhaps he was ill. "Come in," he invited. "You need to eat and to rest." He called for his wife.

Anthony spent two days with the cobbler and asked many questions. The two men became good friends despite Anthony's refusal to say anything about himself. ("It's all right," the cobbler told him. "Whatever has happened, I'm sure that you are a good man. Fortunately, all I do is make sandals. I have nothing to hide.")

When Anthony returned to his cave in the desert, God asked him to describe the sandalmaker.

"He is a simple man, Lord. He has a wife who is expecting a child. He has a small shop, where he makes sandals, and they are made well. He is not rich, but he makes more money than many others in the village. He has faith; he prays at least once every day. He gives money to the poor. He has many friends. He tells jokes. He likes games and parties. He hopes to have many children."

Then God told Anthony that he had been tested and found true. He was a great saint. But the sandalmaker, said God, was as great a saint as Anthony.

I have never prayed to St. Anthony of the Desert, but I have a great devotion to the sandalmaker.

The story illustrates a series of dilemmas that surround the subject of sainthood. First, it is undoubtedly fiction. In the great re-evaluation of Church and faith in the past twenty years, it would be classified as part of the mythology that has passed for so long—far too long—as biography, one of hundreds of legends that have been both a curse and a blessing to our understanding of sanctity. Further, the story states a paradox: a famous saint, who has undergone great tests, is no greater than an ordinary man, an unknown saint, whose holiness appears to have been untested. Anthony knew where he stood in God's sight. The cobbler—who could not get Anthony to talk about himself and who was mercifully untroubled by anyone who sought to teach him about Anthony —did not know how God felt about him. Here the last shall not be first; the last and the first are equal. In one shining legend, the ordinary is revealed, and it is as radiant, as powerful, and as loved as the extraordinary.

Ever since hearing that story, I have venerated unknown saints. I have looked for them in history; I have prayed to them. I know, I know. Such an admission marks me as a Neanderthaler among post-Vatican-II Catholics. Praying to saints, at a time when the statues and votive candles are vanishing from our churches, is embarrassingly unfashionable. Some Catholic friends look upon my peculiar devotion as a childish idiosyncrasy—ignorant or, at best, naïve.

With some heat, they point out that such prayer has been the source of suspicion about us for centuries. We do not need saints, they say, to reach God. They are right. But it may also be true that God uses saints to reach man. In any case, I have always believed that most suspicion is based on misunderstanding. My definition of saints is that they are friends of God. My concept of prayer is conversation. If someone suspects that I commit idolatry when I talk to God's friends, my explanation is that I am only exercising my rights of free speech and peaceful assembly.

I thoroughly agree that it is better to speak to God directly. But I am weak, and I find, at times, that I cannot do it. I do not feel comfortable talking to God about my blocked eustachian tubes or my dislocated kneecap. If this is a spiritual failure, I hope to overcome it. Until then, I am content to talk to the unknown patron saints of these afflictions and to many others to whom I turn in crisis: to the Saint of Bores, of Belches; to the Saint of the Sneeze, the Saint of Malapropisms, the Saint of Solecisms; to The Newest Saint; to departed friends and relatives.

But there is another risk, my friends object: So-and-So may *not* be a saint, after all. My reply is that the recognition of many canonized saints first came through such prayers, and that no prayer is wasted. Indeed the risk, I have pointed out, is not one-sided. Consider the plight of those who prayed to Christopher, who has been stricken entirely from the rolls. I had often prayed to St. Christopher. Many were shocked by his sudden annihilation. For my part, from the moment he became a non-saint—which seems, after all, far more humbling than to be merely unknown—I have prayed to him even more.

Christians live in an ambience of mystery. In all our lives, we are surrounded by an invisible presence, an unprovable reality. Revelations, mystical visions, miracles, are as they were two thousand years ago—rare, almost reluctant manifestations, offered as gifts to create faith or to strengthen weak faith. The greater Christian message remains: love God, whether He offers you miracles or not; love God, whether or not He reveals to you saints who have loved Him. Blessed are those who have not seen and who still believe.

This state of mystery extends even to the disposition of our souls. We believe that to live with God we must be pleasing to God. Are we? To answer seems presumptuous. We are all sinners and can only respond with Joan of Arc, who was asked by her tormentors if her soul was in the state of grace: "If it is not," she replied, "I pray that our Lord will make it so; if it is, I pray that He will preserve me in it."

All saints are unknown until they die. Most remain unknown, but they have been recognized and honored from the earliest days of the Church. St. Paul felt the presence of Old Testament saints as "a cloud of witnesses." We know that the Feast of All Saints, which celebrates Christian saints, known and unknown, was observed at least by the fourth century A.D., around the time when many scholars believe that the concept of a communion of saints was codified in the Apostles' Creed.

The saints who have been canonized, who have received the official ceremony of exaltation in our faith, have not been recognized for the hero-worship that all too often has been given to them. Perhaps, with its elaborate apparatus, its devil's advocate, its demand of miracles, there is no other effort on earth so vulnerable to laughter as the Catholic attempt to measure the immeasurable in the process of canonization. The fact of its long and solemn acceptance is a kind of miracle in itself. But it is hard to remember, once that effort is made, that sainthood did not come to Joan for her political and military achievements, to Ignatius Loyola for his Jesuits, or to Thomas Aquinas for his *Summa*. It came through virtues, after a spiritual warfare that is utterly unknown to us. Occasionally, those virtues are put to a public and final test, but these are spectacular exceptions, unwanted, unsought by any Christian, cups that will not pass. True martyrdom is the daily toil of love, the inner struggle against temptation; true holiness is humble and hidden.

If love is the heart of saintliness, humility is its heartbeat. Again and again, after performing his miracles, Christ instructed that they should not be mentioned. When Pilate looked at Truth and asked, "What is truth?" Christ did not answer. When James and John asked if they could sit next to Christ in Heaven, He explained that among Christians the highest place is reserved for the one who is the servant of all. The Pharisees prayed in public; Christ told us to pray in private.

> When you do an act of charity, do not let your left hand know what your right hand is doing. Your good deed must be secret. . . .

This concept of secrecy, of anonymity, is part of the mystery that makes up our atmosphere, an invisible nimbus that brightens the darkest aspects of life. Evil, for all its stealth, is headlined, photographed, taped; violence, obscenity, lies, seduction, hypocrisy, make up most of our news. But the Christian knows that another record is being kept.

The testaments are filled with nameless people who performed good deeds anonymously: messengers, martyrs, the widow with her mite, the Good Thief and the Good Samaritan, the seventy or seventy-two disciples of whose names we know only that they "are enrolled in Heaven." Ever since, history, between its long passages of the sins of war, politics, and commerce, has given us glimpses of this secret life. They cannot—that is my point—be categorized. But if one looks, the light shines: the unknown builders of the great cathedrals; the anonymous writers of some of the greatest spiritual books: *The Philokalia, The Way of a Pilgrim, The Cloud of Unknowing,* and the work of the man who was known as Bill W., the cofounder of Alcoholics Anonymous, which has touched millions of lives and helped to inspire Al-Anon, Al-

Ateen, Gamblers Anonymous, and scores of therapy programs for drug addicts.

But what of others, well known, who have performed great deeds with great talents? I cannot read Shakespeare, Tolstoy, Dostoevski, I cannot hear Bach, Beethoven, and Mozart, without hoping that they, too, are unknown saints. And what of non-Catholics and non-Christians? I look forward to the day when Catholic ecumenism encourages us to proclaim the sainthood of such men as William Law and Jacob Boehme, two great Protestant contemplatives; of Abu Said ibn Abi l-Khayr, the Persian Sufi master; and Israel, the Baal Shem-Tov, the Polish Jew, founder of modern Hasidism, whose joy and love for God remind me of St. Francis of Assisi.

This is not an original suggestion; I have read of other candidates, including Martin Luther. It would take courage and humility for our Church to make such a gesture, and I pray that it will happen. To whom? To the Patron Saint of Cold Feet, St. Anthony's friend the sandalmaker.

# Biographies
## of the Contributors

### JOHN B. BRESLIN

Born in New York, John Breslin joined the Jesuits in 1961 and studied at Fordham, Oxford (where he received his B.A. and M.A.), and Woodstock, in New York, where he received his M.Div. degree in 1975. After teaching for several years, he was literary editor of *America* in 1971–77 and chairman of the Editorial Board of the Catholic Book Club in 1974–77 and has written numerous articles and reviews for *America*, the New York *Times*, the Washington *Post*, *The New Republic*, and *Commonweal*.

### ROBERT E. BURNS

Executive editor of *U. S. Catholic* magazine and general manager of Claretian Publications, Robert Burns has spent many years in the field of Catholic journalism. He writes reviews and magazine articles and in 1973 received the St. Francis de Sales Award of the Catholic Press Association for "outstanding contributions to Catholic journalism." He is a director of the Thomas More Association and a trustee of Rosary College.

### MARY CARSON

Mary Carson was born and has lived all her life in Baldwin, Long Island. She still lives with her husband, Daniel, and their eight children in the same house in which she was born. Her column "One Mother's View" is syndicated in Catholic papers in the United States and Canada. She has written

numerous book reviews and articles and is the author of
*Ginny*, the moving story of her daughter's near-fatal accident
and the struggle to rehabilitate her. She is much in demand
as an after-dinner speaker and is an active partner in an ad-
vertising business with her husband.

## JOHN DEEDY

Born in Worcester, Massachusetts, John Deedy holds degrees
from Holy Cross and from Trinity College, Dublin. He was a
reporter and correspondent for daily newspapers in Worcester
and Boston and in 1951 decided to devote himself to religious journalism. He was editor of the Worcester diocesan
paper, the *Catholic Free Press*, in 1951–59 and the Pittsburgh diocesan paper, the Pittsburgh *Catholic*, in 1959–67.
He became managing editor of *Commonweal* in 1967, a post
he still holds, writes a column for *Commonweal*, has au-
thored and edited several books, and has contributed articles to
the New York *Times*, *The Critic*, *The New Republic*, and
other journals.

## JOHN J. DELANEY

A real native New Yorker (most native New Yorkers come
from somewhere else), who was born and educated and has
lived all his life in New York, John Delaney has spent his entire career in the book world, the past three decades in Catholic publishing. As editorial director of Doubleday's Catholic
Division, he was responsible for Image Books and the Jerusalem Bible in the United States and has published books by
practically every important Catholic author of the past quarter of a century. He is coauthor of a *Dictionary of Catholic
Biography* and *A Guide to Catholic Reading*, edited the
Catholic Viewpoint and Catholic Perspective series and *A
Woman Clothed with the Sun*, and translated the seventeenth-century spiritual classic *The Practice of the Presence
of God*. He is the recipient of numerous literary awards,
among them the Thomas More Medal, the Campion Award,
and a special Christopher award.

## Anne Fremantle

Born in Aix-les-Bains, France, she was educated at Cheltenham Ladies College and received her M.A. from Oxford. During her distinguished career, she has written for *The Times* of London and the Manchester *Guardian*, ran unsuccessfully for Parliament, and is a regular reviewer for the New York *Times* and the Boston *Herald*. She has served as associate editor for *Commonweal* and the Catholic Book Club, was associate professor at Fordham and taught at City College and New York University, and spent many years with the United Nations. She has contributed articles and short stories to such periodicals as *The New Yorker*, *Vogue*, *Town and Country*, *Harper's Bazaar*, and *The Critic*. She has done extensive radio and television work, made frequent guest appearances, and written her own programs for BBC and NBC. She is a gifted translator, has edited several anthologies, and is the author of a score of books.

## E. E. Y. Hales

An Englishman who spent more than thirty years with the Ministry of Education in London, Edward Hales is well known on both sides of the Atlantic as an outstanding historian. While attending Oxford, he took first-class honors in modern history, has taught at Yale (where he was married to Anne Barnard Porter, an American), and has visited the United States numerous times as lecturer, on a visiting fellowship to the Carnegie Endowment for International Peace, and as Counsellor at the British Embassy in Washington. He has written several outstanding historical works, notably *Pio Nono*, *The Catholic Church in the Modern World*, and *Pope John and his Revolution*, and most recently has turned to fiction with his delightful allegory *Chariot of Fire*.

## Dan Herr

Author, columnist, and publisher, Dan Herr is president of the Thomas More Association, which publishes *The Critic* and hard- and soft-cover books, operates the Thomas More

Book Club, produces Thomas More cassettes, sponsors the Thomas More Book Shop, and publishes the newsletters *Overview, Markings, Sola,* and *For Priests.* A graduate of Fordham, he has also studied at New York, McGill, and Columbia universities. During World War II, he served in the Pacific area, was wounded, and subsequently received the Silver Star. He is the author of *Stop Pushing,* a collection of columns of that title that he writes for *The Critic,* has coedited a half dozen anthologies, including *Bodies and Souls, Blithe Spirits,* and *Moments of Truth,* and writes articles for national magazines. He has served as chairman of the Board of Trustees of Rosary College and is the recipient of an honorary degree, Doctor of Letters *honoris causa,* from Rosary in 1968.

## JOHN S. KENNEDY

A native New Englander who was born and has lived all his life in Hartford, Connecticut, he was educated at St. Thomas Seminary there and the Catholic University in Washington, D.C., where he received his M.A. He was early attracted to journalism, joining the staff of the *Catholic Transcript,* the Hartford diocesan newspaper, soon after his ordination, and has served as editor-in-chief since 1954. He became one of the best-known Catholic literary critics in the United States, and his column, "Balancing the Books," was read by hundreds of thousands in the *Transcript* and *Our Sunday Visitor.* He was made a monsignor in 1955 and was rector of the Hartford cathedral in 1959–71. The author of several books, his *Light on the Mountain* was awarded the Marian Library Medal as the best book on Mary in the year it was published.

## JULIE KERNAN

For three decades before her retirement, in 1966, Julie Kernan was considered one of the outstanding editors in the United States, serving with great distinction at Longmans, Green & Company, David McKay Company, and P. J. Kenedy & Sons. Educated at George Washington University, the

Catholic University in Washington, D.C., and the University of Grenoble, in France, she worked in the international-law division of the Carnegie Endowment for Peace for a decade and was editorial secretary of the French Book Club for several years. She has translated Raïssa Maritain's *We Have Been Friends Together*, François Mauriac's *Life of Christ*, and several lives of the saints, collaborated with Michael Williams on *The Catholic Church in Action*, and is the author of *Our Friend, Jacques Maritain*, her personal memoir of her good friend Jacques Maritain and his wife, Raïssa.

## GLENN D. KITTLER

Glenn Kittler is a free-lance writer whose published magazine articles number over five hundred. He is also the author of more than forty books, including *The White Fathers* and *The Woman God Loved*, a biography of his favorite saint. A native Chicagoan, he attended school there and in Wisconsin, was in the Army during World War II, mostly as a staff writer on the *South Pacific Daily News*, and after the war, worked on newspapers in Chicago and Norfolk before settling in New York to devote himself to writing books and magazine articles. He has been an editor on *Coronet* and is a contributing editor to *Guideposts*, where he also serves as Catholic consultant to Norman Vincent Peale.

## CANDIDA LUND

A Dominican nun, Sister Candida is a native Chicagoan and received her B.A. from Rosary College there and her Ph.D. in political science from the University of Chicago. She served for a time on the research staff of Secretary of the Treasury Henry Morgenthau and then turned to teaching. She became chairman of the Department of Political Science at Rosary in 1961 and has been president of the college since 1964. She has traveled extensively throughout Europe, has written magazine articles, and has received numerous academic awards including a Doctor of Letters *honoris causa* from Lincoln College.

## GARY MACEOIN

Born in Sligo, Ireland, he was educated at the University of London and the National University of Ireland, was admitted to the Dublin bar in 1943 and received his Ph.D. from the National University of Ireland in 1951. He has traveled widely all over the world and is versed in ten languages. He has taught at several universities, has lectured at some fifty universities and colleges in the United States and Canada, and is regarded as an outstanding authority on contemporary Latin America. He has written scores of magazine articles, is the author of a dozen books, makes frequent TV appearances, and has received numerous awards. An American citizen since 1958, he lives with his wife in Tucson, Arizona, but travels extensively, lecturing on matters dealing with world development, Latin America, and the Church.

## THOMAS P. MCDONNELL

A real New Englander, Tom McDonnell was born in Boston, studied journalism at Suffolk University there, and served in the Air Force in World War II. While in England during the war he did some work for the Manchester *Guardian* and on his return home did book reviews for the Boston *Globe* and free-lanced articles for various magazines including *The Critic, America, Commonweal, U. S. Catholic,* and *Catholic World.* Since 1962, he has been book editor and columnist for *The Pilot,* the Boston diocesan newspaper. He writes poetry, was the editor and compiler of the enormously successful *A Thomas Merton Reader,* and in 1975 received the Catholic Press Association Award as the best columnist of the year.

## BARRETT MCGURN

Born in New York, he joined the New York *Herald Tribune* as a reporter after receiving his B.A. from Fordham in 1935. He was a war correspondent in the Pacific during World War II, served as bureau chief for the *Herald Tribune* for sixteen years in Rome, Paris, and Moscow, and on the demise of the *Herald Tribune* was United States Embassy press attaché in Rome in 1966–68. He was United States Embassy counselor for press affairs in Saigon the next year, deputy spokesman for the Department of State from 1969 to 1972, and since then has been director of the Public Information Office of the Supreme Court of the United States. Called "one of the best reporters of religion of our century" by Father John La Farge, he has numerous awards to attest to this judgment and was president of the Overseas Press Club in 1963–65. He has written magazine articles and is the author of *A Reporter Looks at the Vatican* and *A Reporter Looks at American Catholics*.

## FULTON OURSLER, JR.

The son of Fulton Oursler and Grace Perkins, he was born in West Falmouth, Massachusetts, and received his B.A. from Georgetown in 1954. He joined the staff of *Reader's Digest* in 1956, after serving in the Army in 1954–56, and has served as book editor, senior staff member, and since 1974 managing editor. He was married to Anne Nevill in 1954, and they and their five children live in Nyack, New York.

## MARY PURCELL

The daughter of schoolteachers, she was born in Moonveen, Ireland, and taught in Irish schools for three decades. She was assistant editor of the Irish edition of *Messenger of the Sacred Heart* for sixteen years and has lectured and written on religious, historical, and educational themes. Her first book was not published until she was forty, but since then she has had nine biographies published, among them the highly acclaimed *The First Jesuit: St. Ignatius Loyola, Don Francisco,* and *St. Anthony and His Times*; she also wrote a six-book series of religious texts for children. She lives in Dublin and is now writing the life of an Irishman who was a double agent, for the French and for the English, during the French Revolution.

## NAOMI BURTON STONE

Born in Woking, England, Naomi Burton joined the prestigious literary agency Curtis Brown, Ltd., in London after a year of secretarial school. She came to New York in 1939 and eventually became head of the Curtis Brown Book Department here, handling many well-known literary figures, among them Thomas Merton. She became an American citizen in 1945, married Melville Stone in 1951, and in 1955 became a Catholic. After twenty years with Curtis Brown, she joined Doubleday & Company, Inc., in 1959 as a senior editor, and in 1969 left to take an editorial post with the McCall Book Company. Since 1964, when her autobiography *More Than Sentinels* was published, she has lived with her husband at York, Maine, where she is active in CCD work. She lectures and gives courses on religion, is active in liturgical affairs and has served on the board of the Liturgical Conference, and writes a weekly column for *Church World*, Maine's diocesan paper. She is one of the three trustees of Thomas Merton's literary estate, was a close friend and confidante of the Trappist monk before his tragic death in 1968, and is active in promoting further interest in his life and work.

## DONALD J. THORMAN

Born in Oak Park, Illinois, he received his B.A. from De Paul University in 1949 and his M.A. from Loyola University, Chicago, in 1951, and pursued further studies at Michigan, Fribourg, Fordham, and Chicago. He early devoted himself to communications, first with his own business, Catholic Communications Consultants, and then as managing editor of *Voice of St. Jude* (now *U. S. Catholic*), in 1952–56, and managing editor of *Ave Maria* in 1956–62. He taught at Loyola and Fordham and after several years of free-lance writing joined the *National Catholic Reporter* in 1965 as publisher, serving as editor since 1971. He was named president of the NCR Publishing Company, Inc., in 1975. Highly influential in Catholic affairs, Mr. Thorman has lectured widely, appears frequently on radio and TV, has written numerous magazine articles, and is the author of half a dozen books, one of which, *The Emerging Layman*, gave a name to a widespread movement in the Catholic Church.

### TERE RIOS VERSACE

Born in Brooklyn to a Puerto Rican father and an Irish mother, Tere Rios later moved to North Carolina, where she met and married a young army officer, Humbert Versace. With their five children, they lived all over the world, as her husband was sent on various military assignments. In addition to *An Angel Grows Up* and *Brother Angel*, she has had stories and articles published in magazines in the United States and England and is the author of *The Fifteenth Pelican*, which was the basis of the enormously popular TV series "The Flying Nun." She is presently a reporter on a newspaper in Guam.

### JOEL WELLS

Joel Wells is editor of *The Critic* magazine and vice-president of the Thomas More Association in Chicago. He has contributed articles, reviews, and parodies to many publications over the past twenty years. He is also editor of the Thomas More Press, was the author of a number of books, including *Grim Tales for Adults, Under the Spreading Heresy, Second Collection,* and most recently was coauthor with his wife, Betty, of *Here's to the Family.* A graduate of the University of Notre Dame, he lives in Evanston, Illinois, with Betty and their five children.

# OTHER IMAGE BOOKS

ABANDONMENT TO DIVINE PROVIDENCE – Jean Pierre de Caussade. Trans. by John Beevers

AGING: THE FULFILLMENT OF LIFE – Henri J. M. Nouwen and Water J. Gaffney

AND WOULD YOU BELIEVE IT – Bernard Basset, S.J.

APOLOGIA PRO VITA SUA – John Henry Cardinal Newman

AN AQUINAS READER – Ed., with an Intro., by Mary T. Clark

THE ART OF BEING HUMAN – William McNamara, O.C.D.

ASCENT OF MOUNT CARMEL – St. John of the Cross – Trans. and ed. by E. Allison Peers

AUTOBIOGRAPHY OF ST. THÉRÈSE OF LISIEUX: THE STORY OF A SOUL – A new translation by John Beevers

BATTLE FOR THE AMERICAN CHURCH – Msgr. George A. Kelly

BELIEVING – Eugene Kennedy

BIRTH OF THE MESSIAH – Raymond E. Brown

BREAKTHROUGH: MEISTER ECKHART'S CREATION SPIRITUALITY IN NEW TRANSLATION – Matthew Fox

CATHOLIC AMERICA – John Cogley

CENTERING PRAYER – M. Basil Pennington, O.C.S.O.

CHRISTIAN LIFE PATTERNS – Evelyn and James Whitehead

THE CHURCH – Hans Küng

CITY OF GOD – St. Augustine – Ed. by Vernon J. Bourke. Intro. by Étienne Gilson

THE CLOUD OF UNKNOWING (and THE BOOK OF PRIVY COUNSELING) – Newly ed., with an Intro., by William Johnston, S.J.

CLOWNING IN ROME – Henri J. M. Nouwen

A CONCISE HISTORY OF THE CATHOLIC CHURCH (Revised Edition) – Thomas Bokenkotter

THE CONFESSIONS OF ST. AUGUSTINE – Trans., with an Intro., by John K. Ryan

CONJECTURES OF A GUILTY BYSTANDER – Thomas Merton

THE CONSPIRACY OF GOD: THE HOLY SPIRIT IN US – John C. Haughey

CONTEMPLATION IN A WORLD OF ACTION – Thomas Merton

CONTEMPLATIVE PRAYER – Thomas Merton

CREATIVE MINISTRY – Henri J. M. Nouwen

A CRY FOR MERCY – Henri J. M. Nouwen

DAILY WE TOUCH HIM – M. Basil Pennington, O.C.S.O.

DAMIEN THE LEPER – John Farrow

DARK NIGHT OF THE SOUL – St. John of the Cross. Ed. and trans. by E. Allison Peers

# OTHER IMAGE BOOKS

DAWN WITHOUT DARKNESS – Anthony T. Padovano

THE DAYS AND THE NIGHTS – Candida Lund

A DOCTOR AT CALVARY – Pierre Barbet, M.D.

DOORS TO THE SACRED – Joseph Martos

EVERLASTING MAN – G. K. Chesterton

FIRE OF LOVE AND MENDING OF LIFE – Trans., with Intro., by M. L. del Mastro

FLUTE SOLO – Matthew Kelty

THE FOUR GOSPELS: AN INTRODUCTION (Vol. 1) – Bruce Vawter, C.M.

THE FREEDOM OF SEXUAL LOVE – Joseph and Lois Bird

GENESEE DIARY – Henri J. M. Nouwen

GOD LOVE YOU – Fulton J. Sheen

THE GREATEST STORY EVER TOLD – Fulton Oursler

HANS KÜNG: HIS WORK AND HIS WAY – Hermann Häring and Karl-Josef Kuschel

HAS SIN CHANGED? – Seán Fagan

HE LEADETH ME – Walter J. Ciszek, S.J., with Daniel Flaherty, S.J.

THE HERMITAGE JOURNALS – John Howard Griffin

A HISTORY OF PHILOSOPHY: VOLUME 1 – GREECE AND ROME (2 Parts) – Frederick Copleston, S.J.

A HISTORY OF PHILOSOPHY: VOLUME 2 – MEDIAEVAL PHILOSOPHY (2 Parts) – Frederick Copleston, S.J. Part I – Augustine to Bonaventure. Part II – Albert the Great to Duns Scotus

A HISTORY OF PHILOSOPHY: VOLUME 3 – LATE MEDIAEVAL AND RENAISSANCE PHILOSOPHY (2 Parts) – Frederick Copleston, S.J. Part I – Ockham to the Speculative Mystics. Part II – The Revival of Platonism to Suárez

A HISTORY OF PHILOSOPHY: VOLUME 4 – MODERN PHILOSOPHY: Descartes to Leibniz – Frederick Copleston, S.J.

A HISTORY OF PHILOSOPHY: VOLUME 5 – MODERN PHILOSOPHY: The British Philosophers, Hobbes to Hume (2 Parts) – Frederick Copleston, S.J. Part I – Hobbes to Paley. Part II – Berkeley to Hume

A HISTORY OF PHILOSOPHY: VOLUME 6 – MODERN PHILOSOPHY (2 Parts) – Frederick Copleston, S.J. – The French Enlightenment to Kant

A HISTORY OF PHILOSOPHY: VOLUME 7 – MODERN PHILOSOPHY (2 Parts) – Frederick Copleston, S.J. Part I – Fichte to Hegel. Part II – Schopenhauer to Nietzsche

# OTHER IMAGE BOOKS

A HISTORY OF PHILOSOPHY: VOLUME 8 – MODERN PHILOSOPHY: Bentham to Russell (2 Parts) – Frederick Copleston, S.J. Part I – British Empiricism and the Idealist Movement in Great Britain. Part II – Idealism in America, the Pragmatist Movement, the Revolt against Idealism

A HISTORY OF PHILOSOPHY: VOLUME 9 – Maine de Biran to Sartre (2 Parts) – Frederick Copleston, S.J. Part I – The Revolution to Henri Bergson. Part II – Bergson to Sartre

THE IMITATION OF CHRIST – Thomas à Kempis. Ed., with Intro., by Harold C. Gardiner, S.J.

IN SEARCH OF A WAY – Gerard W. Hughes, S.J.

IN SEARCH OF THE BEYOND – Carlo Carretto

INTERIOR CASTLE – St. Teresa of Avila – Trans. and ed. by E. Allison Peers

INTRODUCTION TO THE DEVOUT LIFE – St. Francis de Sales. Trans. and ed. by John K. Ryan

INVITATION TO ACTS – Robert J. Karris

INVITATION TO THE BOOK OF REVELATION – Elisabeth Schüssler Fiorenza

INVITATION TO JOHN – George MacRae

INVITATION TO LUKE – Robert J. Karris

INVITATION TO MARK – Paul J. Achtemeier

INVITATION TO MATTHEW – Donald Senior

INVITATION TO THE NEW TESTAMENT EPISTLES I – Mary Ann Getty

INVITATION TO THE NEW TESTAMENT EPISTLES II – Eugene A. LaVerdiere

INVITATION TO THE NEW TESTAMENT EPISTLES III – Luke Timothy Johnson

INVITATION TO THE NEW TESTAMENT EPISTLES IV – Frederick W. Danker

THE JESUS MYTH – Andrew M. Greeley

JOURNAL OF A SOUL – Pope John XXIII

THE JOY OF BEING HUMAN – Eugene Kennedy

KÜNG IN CONFLICT – Leonard Swidler

LIFE AND HOLINESS – Thomas Merton

LIFE FOR A WANDERER – Andrew M. Greeley

LIFE IS WORTH LIVING – Fulton J. Sheen

THE LIFE OF ALL LIVING – Fulton J. Sheen

LIFE OF CHRIST – Fulton J. Sheen

LIFE OF TERESA OF JESUS: THE AUTOBIOGRAPHY OF ST. TERESA OF AVILA – Trans. and ed. by E. Allison Peers

LIFT UP YOUR HEART – Fulton J. Sheen

LILIES OF THE FIELD – William E. Barrett

# OTHER IMAGE BOOKS

LITTLE FLOWERS OF ST. FRANCIS – Trans. by Raphael Brown
LIVING FLAME OF LOVE – St. John of the Cross. Trans., with Intro., by E. Allison Peers
LIVING IN HOPE – Ladislaus Boros, S.J.
LOURDES: A MODERN PILGRIMAGE – Patrick Marnham
LOVE IS ALL – Joseph and Lois Bird
LOVE IS A COUPLE – Fr. Chuck Gallagher
LOVE TAKES GREATNESS – Fr. Chuck Gallagher
MAN WITH A SONG/Some major and minor notes in the life of Francis of Assisi – Francis and Helen Line
MARRIAGE IS FOR GROWNUPS – Joseph and Lois Bird
MEETING GOD IN MAN – Ladislaus Boros, S.J.
MR. BLUE – Myles Connolly
MODELS OF THE CHURCH – Avery Dulles
MODELS OF JESUS – John F. O'Grady
THE MONASTIC JOURNEY – Thomas Merton
MY LIFE WITH CHRIST – Anthony J. Paone, S.J.
THE NEW SEXUALITY: MYTHS, FABLES AND HANG-UPS – Eugene C. Kennedy
THE NEW TESTAMENT OF THE JERUSALEM BIBLE: Reader's Edition – Alexander Jones, General Editor
THE NEW TESTAMENT OF THE NEW AMERICAN BIBLE (complete and unabridged)
THE OLD TESTAMENT OF THE JERUSALEM BIBLE: Reader's Edition – Alexander Jones, General Editor
  Volume 2: 1 Samuel – 2 Maccabees; Volume 3: Job – Ecclesiasticus; Volume 4: The Prophets – Malachi
THE OLD TESTAMENT WITHOUT ILLUSION – John L. McKenzie
ON BEING HUMAN – Fulton J. Sheen
ORTHODOXY – G. K. Chesterton
OUR LADY OF FATIMA – William Thomas Walsh
THE PAIN OF BEING HUMAN – Eugene Kennedy
PARENTS ARE LOVERS – Fr. Chuck Gallagher
PEACE OF SOUL – Fulton J. Sheen
THE PERFECT JOY OF ST. FRANCIS – Felix Timmermans. Trans. by Raphael Brown
POCKET DICTIONARY OF SAINTS – John J. Delaney
POPE JOHN PAUL II: THE LIFE OF KAROL WOJTYLA – Mieczyslaw Malinski
THE POWER OF LOVE – Fulton J. Sheen
POWER TO THE PARENTS! – Joseph and Lois Bird
THE PRACTICE OF THE PRESENCE OF GOD – Trans. with an Intro. by John J. Delaney

# OTHER IMAGE BOOKS

THE PSALMS OF THE JERUSALEM BIBLE — Alexander Jones, General Editor

A RELIGIOUS HISTORY OF THE AMERICAN PEOPLE (2 vols.) — Sydney E. Ahlstrom

RENEWING THE EARTH — Ed. by David J. O'Brien and Thomas A. Shannon

REVELATIONS OF DIVINE LOVE — Trans. with an Intro. by M. L. del Mastro

THE RULE OF ST. BENEDICT — Trans. and ed., with an Intro., by Anthony C. Meisel and M. L. del Mastro

ST. FRANCIS OF ASSISI — G. K. Chesterton

ST. FRANCIS OF ASSISI — Johannes Jorgensen

SAINT THOMAS AQUINAS — G. K. Chesterton

SAINTS ARE NOW — John J. Delaney

SAINTS FOR ALL SEASONS — John J. Delaney, editor

THE SCREWTAPE LETTERS (Illus.) — C. S. Lewis

A SENSE OF LIFE, A SENSE OF SIN — Eugene Kennedy

SHOULD ANYONE SAY FOREVER? — John C. Haughey

THE SHROUD OF TURIN (Revised Edition) — Ian Wilson

THE SINAI MYTH — Andrew M. Greeley

SOMETHING BEAUTIFUL FOR GOD — Malcolm Muggeridge

THE SPIRIT OF CATHOLICISM — Karl Adam

THE SPIRITUAL EXERCISES OF ST. IGNATIUS — Trans. by Anthony Mottola, Ph.D. Intro. by Robert W. Gleason, S.J.

THE STAIRWAY OF PERFECTION — Trans. and ed. by M. L. del Mastro

STORM OF GLORY — John Beevers

THE STORY OF THE TRAPP FAMILY SINGERS — Maria Augusta Trapp

SUFFERING — Louis Evely

SUMMA THEOLOGIAE — Thomas Aquinas. General Editor: Thomas Gilby, O.P.

   Volume 1: The Existence of God. Part One: Questions 1-13

A THEOLOGY OF THE OLD TESTAMENT — John L. McKenzie

THE THIRD PEACOCK — Robert Farrar Capon

THIRSTING FOR THE LORD — Carroll Stuhlmueller

THIS MAN JESUS — Bruce Vawter

THOMAS MERTON — Cornelia and Irving Sussman

THOMAS MERTON ON MYSTICISM — Raymond Bailey

THOMAS MERTON ON PRAYER — John J. Higgins, S.J.

A THOMAS MERTON READER — Revised Edition — Ed. by Thomas P. McDonnell

A TIME FOR LOVE — Eugene C. Kennedy

TO LIVE AS FAMILY — Joseph and Lois Bird

# OTHER IMAGE BOOKS

TOWARD A NEW CATHOLIC MORALITY – John Giles Milhaven

TREASURE IN CLAY – The Autobiography of Fulton J. Sheen

TURNING/Reflections on the Experience of Conversion – Emilie Griffin

UNDERSTANDING MYSTICISM – Ed. by Richard Woods, O.P.

THE WAY OF PERFECTION – St. Teresa of Avila. Trans. and ed. by E. Allison Peers

THE WAY OF A PILGRIM (AND THE PILGRIM CONTINUES HIS WAY) – Trans. by Helen Bacovcin

WE ARE ALL BROTHERS – Louis Evely

WHY CATHOLIC? – Ed. by John J. Delaney

THE WIT AND WISDOM OF BISHOP FULTON J. SHEEN – Ed. by Bill Adler

WITH GOD IN RUSSIA – Walter J. Ciszek, S.J., with Daniel L. Flaherty, S.J.

A WOMAN CLOTHED WITH THE SUN – Ed. by John J. Delaney

THE WORLD'S FIRST LOVE – Fulton J. Sheen

THE WOUNDED HEALER – Henri J. M. Nouwen

YOUR CATHOLIC WEDDING: A Complete Plan-Book – Rev. Chris Aridas

A 83 – 6